SECRETS
• *from the* •
LA VARENNE
KITCHEN

50 ESSENTIAL RECIPES
EVERY COOK NEEDS TO KNOW

SECRETS
• *from the* •
LA VARENNE
KITCHEN

50 ESSENTIAL RECIPES
EVERY COOK NEEDS TO KNOW

ANNE WILLAN

Founder of the Legendary Cooking School
Ecole de Cuisine La Varenne

SPRING HOUSE PRESS

www.lavarenne.com

Secrets from the La Varenne Kitchen (2015)

Publisher: Paul McGahren
Editor: Matthew Teague
Designer: Lindsay Hess
Assistant editors: Tina Kil, Nicole Quessenberry
Copyeditor: Marcia Ryan
Indexer: Holly Day

This edition is based on the book given to all
students at Ecole de Cuisine La Varenne:

La Varenne Basic Recipes (1978)

Editors: Anne Willan, Faye Levy
Assistant editors: Nancy Dalrymple
                   Lauren Kaye
                   Nina Simonds
Layout: Tiggi Wood
Recipe testing: Bruce Weller

The illustrations in this book are taken from Jules Gouffé's
Le Livre de Cuisine published in 1867.

Spring House Press
3613 Brush Hill Court
Nashville, TN 37216

ISBN: 978-1-940611-15-0
Library of Congress Control Number: 2014953154
Printed in China
First Printing: April 2015

To learn more about Spring House Press books, or to find a
retailer near you, email *info@springhousepress.com* or visit
us at *www.springhousepress.com*.

INTRODUCTION

How reassuring it is that the fundamentals of good cooking are constant. Nearly forty years ago, in the early days of La Varenne Cooking School, we were issuing sheaves of background recipes to our students. Out of necessity, we compiled *La Varenne Basic Recipes*. In this one small book of 50 recipes the students had all they needed to begin cooking.

I never thought these fundamentals would remain the same today. Here in *Secrets from the La Varenne Kitchen*, the measurements and simple instructions are exactly the same as in *Basic Recipes*. The French version created to guide our chefs at La Varenne in Paris is even more relevant now that metrics are spreading the globe. As for the charming illustrations dating back to 1867, the pots and pans, the spoons and whisks, and many of the gadgets remain identical today.

Think of the mother sauces—we all still relish a buttery, fresh hollandaise sauce or a homemade aioli. The foundation pastry doughs—pie pastry, choux, and puff—have not changed in hundreds of years. After a brief decline, glittering white meringues are back on the plate, while sherbets and ice creams remain a sure-fire staple. What I secretly yearn for is one of those dark, rich, glossy brown espagnole sauces that add such depth to meats, particularly beef. Too good to miss, they are bound to return!

I've asked several of our long-term students and trainees from La Varenne, many of them now well-known names in the food world, just why they think the original booklet and the recipes it contains are so important. A few of their comments are printed on the following pages.

The foundations of good cooking are ageless!

Anne Willan

FROM THE STUDENTS *of* LA VARENNE COOKING SCHOOL

"I'm a cookbook accumulator—I have more than 1,000, all well chosen for their excellent contents and designs. But do I cook from any of them? Very rarely! There is one exception, however, and it's a scruffy little book that was given to me when I was a student at La Varenne: the *Basic Recipes* book. My copy is more than 25 years old now and has a few stained pages, due to the fact that I find myself referring to it for just about every recipe development project I've done."

> —**Martha Holmberg**, former editor and publisher of *Fine Cooking* magazine, founding editor of MIX magazine, and author of *Modern Sauces*

"My copy of *La Varenne Basic Recipes* which I was given when I first arrived at Château du Feÿ as a stagiaire, in 1989, still sits at eye level on my cookbook shelves. It's an excellent quick reference for the kind of detail that can slip any cook's mind. "What's the correct temperature for caramel, again?" "Why was it I'm not supposed to boil the fish stock?" The book is full of tricks that take good cooking to great, along with recipes which form the essential foundation of any home cook's repertoire. I'd be lost without it."

> —**Laura Calder**, James Beard award-winner, best-selling cookbook author, and host of *French Food at Home*

"This is the only book that I've kept at my side for over 20 years that still triggers perfection and inspires me to master beautiful technique. For any level of cook or chef, this book is a must-have reference to basics or advanced skills to remind us always what it was and what it's supposed to be!"

> —**Ana Sortun**, James Beard award-winning Mediterranean chef and owner of Oleana in Cambridge, Mass.

"The La Varenne recipes remain indispensible to me in my culinary career, and *Basic Recipes* is my go-to when recreating any of the classic French dishes. Once a cook masters these 50 recipes, he or she will have gained a very firm foundation, indeed."

> – **Anna Watson Carl**, author of *The Yellow Table:*
> *A Celebration of Everyday Gatherings*

"This compact booklet holds the key that unlocks the secrets to making basic stocks, French sauces, and indispensable pastry components. If you can have only one basic book, this is it!"

> —**Gale Gand**, co-founder of Spritz Burger and Tru,
> best-selling author of *Gale Gand's Lunch!* and
> two-time James Beard award-winning pastry chef

"La Varenne founder Anne Willan taught a generation of Americans how to cook. This timeless reference book has been my go-to guide for the fundamentals of French cuisine since my student days in Paris. It remains an indispensable resource for any serious student of the culinary arts."

> —**Steven Raichlen**, James Beard award winning author,
> grilling authority, and host of *Primal Grill* on PBS

"There are few books more well-worn than my tattered copy of *La Varenne Basic Recipes*. It's my go-to guide for foundation recipes. There are hundreds if not hundreds of thousands of these sorts of recipes in print and on the internet, but I am certain that these work and work well. La Varenne and Anne Willan continually guide me in the kitchen and in my food writing nearly each and every day. I am a better cook and writer because of it."

> —**Virginia Willis**, Southern food authority, chef, and
> best selling cookbook author of *Bon Appétit, Y'all*

INTRODUCTION *from* *the* ORIGINAL EDITION, *LA VARENNE BASIC RECIPES (1975)*

This basic recipe book has been developed under the most exacting of test conditions—the daily practical classes at Ecole de Cuisine La Varenne in Paris. The recipes have been used constantly by students at all levels of expertise for nearly three years and this new, expanded edition builds on their experience. La Varenne's three French chefs, *cuisiniers* Fernand Chambrette and Claude Vauguet, and *pâtissier* Albert Jorant, have been the guiding light in making what we hope will be an indispensable reference for teachers as well as students of French cooking.

Ingredient quantities in English are given in U.S. standard measures and are intended for use in North America, Japan, Australia, and wherever flour is made from hard wheat with a high gluten content. Metric measures, listed in French, are designed for Europe, where flour is softer, yielding doughs with less elasticity.

This is not a book of finished dishes, though some recipes such as sherbet are complete in themselves. Rather it is a collection of the sauces, pastries, and creams that go to make up a dish. Above all, this is a working tool, to fashion professional excellence. It is a practical book for practical cooks.

Pasta. *Pâtes.*

Vegetables. *Légumes.*

CONTENTS

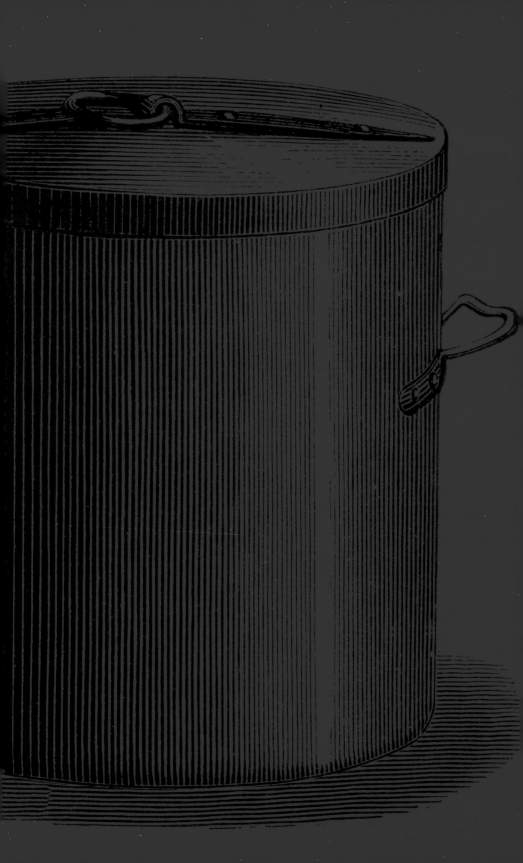

CHAPTER 1

STOCKS AND ASPIC

Les Fonds et la Gelée

French savory cooking begins with stocks
(the French word *fond* means "foundation").
Stock is the first lesson in the La Varenne
kitchen, essential to many soups, stews,
and sauces. When stock is clarified with
egg white and flavorings of chopped
vegetables, it becomes aspic, the
subject of more advanced classes.

BROWN VEAL STOCK
Fond Brun de Veau

4-5 pounds of veal bones, cracked or cut in small pieces
2 onions, quartered
2 carrots, quartered
2 stalks celery, cut in 2-inch pieces
1 large bouquet garni
10 peppercorns
1 head garlic, split, with skin on
1 tablespoon tomato paste
3-4 quarts water

Brown veal stock is used for brown sauces and for rich ragoûts and braised dishes.

Makes 2-3 quarts stock.

> *2 kg d'os de veau, concassés*
> *2 oignons, coupés en quartiers*
> *2 carottes, coupées en quartiers*
> *2 branches de céleri, coupées en morceaux de 5 cm*
> *1 gros bouquet garni*
> *10 grains de poivre*
> *1 tête d'ail non épluchée, coupée en deux*
> *1 cuiller à soupe de concentré de tomate*
> *3-4 litres d'eau*
>
> *Le fond brun de veau est destiné à mouiller des sauces brunes, des ragoûts riches, et des braises.*
>
> *Rendement: 2-3 litres de fond.*

Put the cracked bones in a roasting pan and roast in a very hot oven (450°F) for 30-40 minutes, or until the bones are browned, stirring them occasionally. Add the vegetables and brown them also. Transfer the bones and vegetables to a stock pot with a metal spoon, leaving the fat behind. Add the bouquet garni, peppercorns, garlic, tomato paste, and water and bring slowly to a boil. Skim often at first, then simmer the stock for 4-5 hours, skimming occasionally; it should reduce very slowly. To add color to the stock, singe half a cut onion over an electric plate or gas burner and add to the stock.

Strain the stock, taste and if the flavor is not concentrated, boil it until well reduced. Chill quickly by placing the pot of stock in running cold water and skim off any fat before using. Stock can be kept 2-3 days in the refrigerator. To keep it longer, boil it for 5-10 minutes and then chill again. It can also be frozen.

Stock pots. *Marmites.*

BROWN BEEF STOCK
Fond Brun de Boeuf

Beef stock is used for rich sauces and game dishes. Substitute beef bones for half of the veal bones. Beef stock has a more mellow flavor than brown veal stock, but it is less syrupy because it contains less gelatin.

WHITE VEAL STOCK
Fond Blanc de Veau

White veal stock is used for lighter sauces to serve with veal and poultry. Follow the recipe for brown veal stock but do not brown the bones or vegetables and omit the tomato paste. Blanch the bones by bringing them to a boil in water to cover, simmering 5 minutes, draining, and rinsing in cold water. Then make the stock with vegetables, flavorings, and water, as for brown veal stock.

Copper stock pot. *Marmite en cuivre.*

CHICKEN STOCK
Fond de Volaille

3 pounds chicken backs and necks or a whole fowl

1.5 kg d'os et de carcasses de volaille ou 1 poule

For poultry dishes and sauces. Follow the recipe for white veal stock, substituting 3 pounds chicken backs and necks or a whole fowl for half the veal bones. Simmer the stock 3-4 hours or, if using a fowl, remove it after about 1½ hours or when the thigh is tender when pierced with a skewer. Serve the fowl cold or use it in some other dish.

CHICKEN STOCK *for* CONSOMME *and* ASPIC
Fond de Volaille pour Consommé ou Gelée

3 pounds raw chicken bones or a small fowl

1.5 kg d'os crus de volaille ou 1 poule

Follow the recipe for white veal stock, adding 3 pounds raw chicken bones or a small fowl to the 5 pounds veal bones.

FISH STOCK
Fumet de Poisson

1 medium onion, sliced
1 tablespoon butter
1½ pounds fish bones, broken into pieces
1 quart water
10 peppercorns
1 bouquet garni
1 cup dry white wine or juice ½ lemon (optional)

Makes about 1 quart stock.

> *1 oignon de taille moyenne, emincé*
> *15 g de beurre*
> *750 g d'arêtes de poisson, coupées en morceaux*
> *1 litre d'eau*
> *10 grains de poivre*
> *1 bouquet garni*
> *2.5 dl de vin blanc sec ou le jus d'un ½ citron (facultatif)*
>
> *Rendement: 1 litre de fumet environ.*

In a kettle, sauté the onion in the butter until the onion is soft but not brown. Add the fish bones, water, peppercorns, bouquet garni, and wine or lemon juice if used. Bring slowly to a boil, skimming occasionally, and simmer 20 minutes, uncovered. Strain and season to taste. **NOTE:** Never boil fish stock or it will become bitter. Do not add fish skin to the stock as this darkens it.

COURT BOUILLON
Court Bouillon

1 quart water
1 carrot, sliced
1 small onion, sliced
1 bouquet garni
6 peppercorns
1 teaspoon salt
1 cup white wine or ⅓ cup vinegar or ¼ cup lemon juice

Makes 1 quart court bouillon.

> *1 litre d'eau*
> *1 carotte, emincée*
> *1 petit oignon, coupé en tranches*
> *1 bouquet garni*
> *6 grains de poivre noir*
> *1 cuiller à café de sel*
> *2.5 dl de vin blanc sec, 1 dl de vinaigre ou 6.5 cl de jus de citron*
>
> *Rendement: 1 litre de court bouillon.*

Combine all the ingredients in a pan (not aluminum), cover and bring to a boil. Simmer uncovered 15-20 minutes and strain.

Bowl of broth. *Bol à bouillon.*

MEAT GLAZE
Glace de Viande

Meat glaze is used in very small quantities to add body to sauces and ragoûts. It sets very firmly and can be kept several months uncovered in the refrigerator.

Method 1

Boil brown veal stock until very reduced, dark and syrupy in consistency. As it reduces, change to smaller saucepans and lower the heat to avoid scorching.

3 quarts of stock make about 1 cup of glaze.

Method 2

Put the bones and vegetables strained from brown veal stock into a stock pot, cover with water, and simmer 4-5 hours until very reduced and 2-3 cups liquid remain. Strain, reduce further until syrupy, and let cool.

FISH GLAZE
Glace de Poisson

Boil fish stock until very reduced, dark and syrupy in consistency. Use in very small quantities to add body to fish sauces. Keep as for meat glaze.

3 quarts of stock make about 1 cup of glaze.

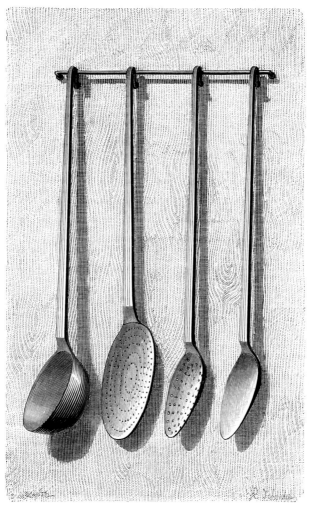

Spoons and skimmers. *Cuillers et écumoires.*

MEAT *or* FISH ASPIC
Gelée de Viande ou de Poisson

1½ quarts well flavored beef, veal, chicken, or fish stock
2-4 envelopes gelatin (optional)
Red and yellow food coloring (optional)
Salt and pepper
2 carrots, chopped
Green tops of 2 leeks, chopped
2 stalks celery, chopped
2 tomatoes, quartered
7 ounces finely chopped lean beef (for meat aspic)
    or finely chopped fish (for fish aspic)
3 egg whites, beaten until frothy
¼ cup Madeira or sherry

Makes about 1 quart aspic.

1.5 litres de bon fond de boeuf, de veau, de volaille, ou de poisson
15-30 g de gélatine (facultatif)
Colorant végétal rouge et jaune (facultatif)
Sel et poivre
2 carottes, hachées
Les parties vertes de 2 poireaux, hachées
2 branches de céleri, hachées
2 tomates, coupées en quatre
200 g de boeuf maigre haché (pour gelée de viande)
    ou de poisson haché (pour gelée de poisson)
3 blancs d'oeufs, légèrement battus
6.5 cl de Madère ou de Xérès

Rendement: 1 litre de gelée environ.

The stock must be firmly set. If not, add 2-4 envelopes gelatin, depending if it is lightly set or almost liquid and on how soon you need it. Sprinkle the gelatin over ½ cup of the stock in a small bowl and leave 5 minutes or until spongy.

Skim all the fat from the stock, heat it slightly in a large pan (not aluminum), and remove any remaining fat with strips of paper towel. If necessary, color the stock with a few drops of red and yellow food coloring. Fish aspic can be almost colorless, veal and chicken should be light gold, and beef aspic for red meats and game should be a rich golden brown. In a bowl thoroughly mix the carrots, leeks, celery, tomatoes, chopped beef or fish, and egg whites. Pour on the warm stock and return to the pan. Set the pan over moderate heat and bring slowly to a boil, whisking constantly—this should take about 10 minutes.

When the mixture looks milky at once stop whisking. **NOTE:** Whisking further prevents the formation of the filter. Let the filter of egg whites rise slowly to the top of the pan, and then turn down the heat. With a ladle make a small hole in the egg white filter, so the aspic bubbles through the filter only in that place; otherwise the filter may break.

Let the aspic simmer gently for 30-40 minutes to extract the flavor from the vegetables and meat or fish and to allow the liquid to strain through the egg white filter. Carefully add the gelatin through the hole in the filter; simmer gently for 2-3 minutes to be sure it is dissolved. Taste the aspic for seasoning and add the Madeira or sherry.

Place a scalded dish towel or jelly bag in a strainer over a clean bowl and ladle the aspic and egg white filter into it, beginning where the hole was made. Do not press on the vegetables, meat, or fish left in the towel. If the aspic running through is not sparkling clear, strain it again through the cloth and filter. Leave it to cool.

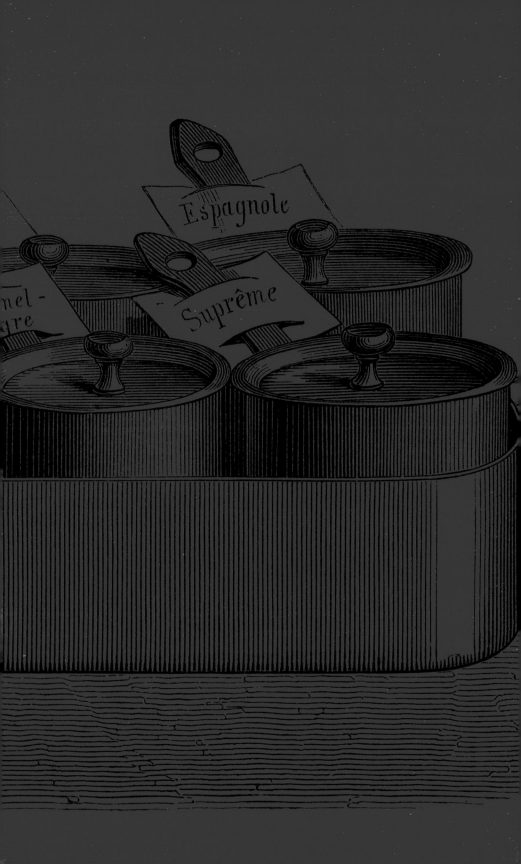

CHAPTER 2

HOT AND COLD SAUCES

Les Sauces Froides et Chaudes

The most famous French sauces are called "mothers" (*mères*) because they lead to dozens of variations. Espagnole and Velouté are based on beef, veal, chicken, or fish stock. Other mother sauces include Béchamel, Hollandaise, Béarnaise, and White Butter Sauces.

In class at La Varenne Cooking School, mothers lead to derivatives such as Sauce Bordelaise (Espagnole with white wine and shallot), Sauce Périgueux (Espagnole with Madeira and truffles), mayonnaise-based Sauce Remoulade and many more.

ESPAGNOLE SAUCE
Sauce Espagnole

4 tablespoons oil
3 ounce piece of smoked bacon, diced
1 onion, diced
1 carrot, diced
5 tablespoons flour
4 cups brown veal stock
1 bouquet garni
1 tomato, quartered
1 tablespoon tomato paste
Salt and pepper

Makes about 3 cups sauce.

4 chillers à soup d'huile
90 g de poitrine fumée, coupée en dés
1 oignon, coupé en dés
1 carotte, coupée en dés
50 g de farine
1 litre de fond brun de veau
1 bouquet garni
1 tomate, coupée en quatre
1 cuiller à soupe de concentré de tomate
Sel et poivre

Rendement: 7.5 dl de sauce environ.

In a heavy based pan, heat the oil. Add the bacon, onion, and carrot and sauté until lightly browned. Add the flour and cook, stirring with a wooden spoon, until the mixture is a rich brown. Take from the heat and let cool. Heat three cups of the brown stock and, when hot, whisk into the cooled roux. Add the bouquet garni, tomato, and tomato paste and bring the mixture to a boil, stirring constantly. Let it simmer very gently, uncovered for 3 hours or until thoroughly reduced and well flavored. It should be quite red, with a strong flavor of tomato and an almost syrupy consistency. To clarify the sauce: Once or twice during cooking add half a cup of stock, bring the sauce back to a boil, and skim off any scum. Strain the sauce through a chinois strainer and taste it for seasoning. Use as a base for other brown sauces.

Pointed sauce strainer. *Passoire dite chinois.*

BASIC BROWN SAUCE
Fond de Veau Lié

3 cups well-flavored brown veal stock
2 tablespoons arrowroot or potato starch
4 tablespoons Madeira or water
Salt and pepper

Makes about 3 cups sauce.

> *7.5 dl de fond brun de veau, bien réduit*
> *2 cuillers à soupe d'arrowroot ou de fécule*
> *4 cuillers à soupe de Madère ou d'eau*
> *Sel et poivre*
>
> *Rendement: 7.5 dl de sauce environ.*

Bring the stock to a boil. Mix the arrowroot or potato starch to a paste with the Madeira or cold water. Pour the mixture into the stock, whisking constantly, adding enough to thicken the sauce to the desired consistency. Bring it back to a boil, taste for seasoning, and strain through a fine strainer. Use as a base for other brown sauces.

Large copper colander. *Grande passoire en cuivre.*

BROWN SAUCE DERIVATIVES
Dérivés de Sauces Brunes

Sauce Bercy

2 finely chopped shallots
½ cup white wine
2 cups basic brown sauce

> *2 échalottes, finement hachées*
> *1.25 dl de vin blanc*
> *5 dl de fond de veau lié*

Reduce 2 finely chopped shallots and ½ cup white wine to about 2 tablespoons. Stir in 2 cups basic brown sauce and taste for seasoning. Serve with veal.

Sauce Bordelaise

2 finely chopped shallots
¼ teaspoon freshly ground black pepper
1 cup red wine
2 cups espagnole sauce or basic brown sauce
Marrow from 2 marrow bones, scooped out with a knife dipped in hot water, sliced, poached for 1-2 minutes in simmering water, and drained

> *2 échalottes, finement hachées*
> *¼ cuiller à café de poivre noir fraîchement moulu*
> *2.5 dl de vin rouge*
> *5 dl de sauce espagnole ou de fond de veau lié*
> *La moelle pochée de 2 os de boeuf*

Reduce 2 finely chopped shallots and ¼ teaspoon freshly ground black pepper with 1 cup red wine to about ½ cup. Strain and add to 2 cups espagnole sauce or basic brown sauce. Bring just back to a boil and taste for seasoning. Add the marrow from 2 marrow bones, which has been scooped out with a knife dipped in hot water, sliced, poached for 1-2 minutes in simmering water, and drained. Serve with roast beef and steak, particularly entrecôte.

BROWN SAUCE DERIVATIVES *(continued)*
Dérivés de Sauces Brunes *(suite)*

Sauce Bretonne

½ onion, finely chopped
2 tablespoons butter
1 cup white wine
1 cup espagnole sauce or basic brown sauce
1 cup tomato sauce or 2 tablespoons tomato paste
1 clove garlic, crushed
2 teaspoons chopped parsley

> *½ oignon, finement haché*
> *30 g de beurre*
> *2.5 dl de vin blanc*
> *2.5 dl de sauce espagnole ou de fond de veau lié*
> *2.5 dl de sauce tomate ou 2 cuillers à soupe de concentré de tomate*
> *1 gousse d'ail écrasée*
> *2 cuillers à café de persil haché*

Sauté ½ onion, finely chopped, in 2 tablespoons butter until soft, but not browned. Add 1 cup white wine and reduce by half. Add 1 cup espagnole sauce or basic brown sauce, 1 cup tomato sauce or 2 tablespoons tomato paste, and 1 clove garlic, crushed. Simmer 8-10 minutes, taste for seasoning, and add 2 teaspoons chopped parsley. Serve with roast lamb, particularly when accompanied by dried haricot beans.

Sauce Charcutière

⅔ cup white wine
⅓ cup white wine vinegar
2 finely chopped shallots
2 cups espagnole sauce or basic brown sauce
3 gherkin pickles cut in julienne strips

> *2 dl de vin blanc*
> *1 dl de vinaigre de vin blanc*
> *2 échalottes, finement hachées*
> *5 dl de sauce espagnole ou de fond de veau lié*
> *3 cornichons*

Reduce ⅔ cup white wine, ⅓ cup white wine vinegar, and 2 finely chopped shallots to about 2 tablespoons. Add 2 cups espagnole sauce or basic brown sauce with 3 gherkin pickles cut in julienne strips and taste for seasoning. Serve with pork.

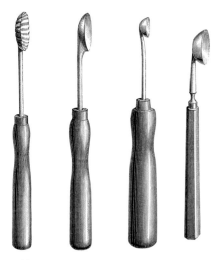

Vegetable spoons. *Cuillers à légumes.*

BROWN SAUCE DERIVATIVES *(continued)*
Dérivés de Sauces Brunes (suite)

Sauce Chasseur

2 shallots, finely chopped
2 tablespoons butter
¼ pound mushrooms, thinly sliced
1 cup white wine
1 cup basic brown sauce
1 cup tomato sauce or 2 tablespoons tomato paste
2 tablespoons butter in small pieces
1 tablespoon chopped parsley
2 teaspoons chopped tarragon

> *2 échalottes, finement hachées*
> *30 g de beurre*
> *125 g de champignons, finement émincés*
> *2.5 dl de vin blanc*
> *2.5 dl de fond de veau lié*
> *2.5 dl de sauce tomate ou 2 cuillers à soupe de concentré de tomate*
> *30 g de beurre*
> *1 cuiller à soupe de persil haché*
> *2 cuillers à café d'estragon haché*

Sauté 2 shallots, finely chopped, in 2 tablespoons butter until soft.
Add ¼ pound mushrooms, thinly sliced, and cook until soft. Add 1 cup
white wine and reduce to about ⅓ cup. Add 1 cup basic brown sauce
and 1 cup tomato sauce or 2 tablespoons tomato paste, and bring
just back to a boil. Take from the heat and whisk in 2 tablespoons
butter in small pieces, 1 tablespoon chopped parsley, and if you like,
2 teaspoons chopped tarragon. Taste for seasoning and do not reboil.
Serve with all broiled or roast meats, chicken, and rabbit.

Sauce Demi-Glace

2 cups espagnole sauce or basic brown sauce
4 tablespoons chopped mushrooms
2 teaspoons tomato paste
¼ cup veal or beef stock
¼ cup Madeira
2 tablespoons butter in pieces

> *5 dl de sauce espagnole ou de fond de veau lié*
> *50 g de champignons hachés*
> *2 cuillers à café de concentré de tomate*
> *6.5 cl fond de veau ou de boeuf*
> *6.5 cl de Madère*
> *30 g de beurre*

To 2 cups espagnole sauce or basic brown sauce add 4 tablespoons chopped mushrooms, 2 teaspoons tomato paste, ¼ cup veal or beef stock, and ¼ cup Madeira. Simmer, skimming often until reduced to about 2 cups, take from the heat and taste for seasoning. Whisk in 2 tablespoons butter in pieces. Demi-glace is served with meats and can be a base for other sauces.

Hand position for trimming mushrooms.
Position des mains pour tourner les champignons.

BROWN SAUCE DERIVATIVES *(continued)*
Dérivés de Sauces Brunes *(suite)*

Sauce Diable

½ cup white wine
½ cup white wine vinegar
2 shallots, finely chopped
2 teaspoons tomato paste
2 cups espagnole sauce or basic brown sauce
Touch of cayenne

1.25 dl de vin blanc
1.25 dl de vinaigre de vin blanc
2 échalottes, finement hachées
2 cuillers à café de concentré de tomate
5 dl de sauce espagnole ou de fond de veau lié
Pincée de cayenne

Reduce ½ cup white wine, ½ cup white wine vinegar, 2 shallots, finely chopped, and 2 teaspoons tomato paste to about ⅓ cup. Add 2 cups espagnole sauce or basic brown sauce and bring to a boil. Take from the heat and add a touch of cayenne. Taste for seasoning and do not reboil. Serve with roast and broiled meats and chicken.

Sauce Italienne

½ onion, chopped
1 tablespoon butter
¼ pound mushrooms, chopped
1 cup white wine
2 cups espagnole sauce or basic brown sauce
2 oz cooked lean ham, cut in small cubes

½ oignon haché
15 g de beurre
125 g de champignons hachés
2.5 dl de vin blanc
5 dl de sauce espagnole ou de fond de veau lié
60 g de jambon maigre cuit

Sauté ½ onion, chopped, in 1 tablespoon butter until soft but not brown. Add ¼ pound mushrooms, chopped, and cook until soft. Add 1 cup white wine and reduce to ½ cup. Stir in 2 cups espagnole sauce or basic brown sauce, bring to a boil, and add 2 oz cooked lean ham cut in small cubes. Taste for seasoning. Serve with roast beef, steak, and veal.

BROWN SAUCE DERIVATIVES *(continued)*
Dérivés de Sauces Brunes (suite)

Sauce Madère

3 tablespoons Madeira (or to taste)
2 cups demi-glace sauce

◄ OR ►

3 tablespoons Madeira (or to taste)
2 cups espagnole sauce, or basic brown sauce
Additional 3 tablespoons Madeira (or to taste)

> *3 cuillers à soupe de Madère*
> *5 dl de sauce demi-glace*
>
> ◄ *OU* ►
>
> *3 cuillers à soupe de Madère*
> *5 dl de sauce espagnole ou de fond de veau lié*
> *Si nécessaire, 3 cuillers à soupe de Madère en plus*

Add 3 tablespoons Madeira (or to taste) to 2 cups demi-glace sauce and bring just to a boil. Alternatively, simmer 3 tablespoons Madeira with 2 cups espagnole sauce or basic brown sauce for 8-10 minutes, add 3 tablespoons more Madeira (or to taste), and bring just back to a boil. Serve with variety meats, beef filet, veal, and ham.

Sauce Périgueux

Juice from 1 small can truffles
2 cups demi-glace sauce
Truffles, diced

◄ OR ►

3 tablespoons Madeira
Juice from 1 small can truffles
2 cups espagnole sauce or basic brown sauce
Truffles, diced

> *Le jus d'une petite boîte de truffes*
> *5 dl de sauce demi-glace*
> *Les truffes coupées en dés*
>
> *◄ OU ►*
>
> *3 cuillers à soupe de Madère*
> *Le jus d'une petite boîte de truffes*
> *5 dl de sauce espagnole ou de fond de veau lié*
> *Les truffes coupées en dés*

Add the juice from 1 small can truffles to 2 cups demi-glace sauce, bring to a boil, and add the truffles, diced. Alternatively, simmer 3 tablespoons Madeira and the juice from 1 small can truffles with 2 cups espagnole sauce or basic brown sauce for 8-10 minutes, add the diced truffles, and taste for seasoning. Serve with beef filet, ham, veal, and egg dishes.

BROWN SAUCE DERIVATIVES *(continued)*
Dérivés de Sauces Brunes (suite)

Sauce Piquante

½ cup white wine
½ cup white wine vinegar
2 chopped shallots
2 cups espagnole sauce
2 tablespoons coarsely chopped gherkin pickles
1 tablespoon chopped parsley
2 teaspoons chopped tarragon
2 teaspoons chopped chervil

> *1.25 dl de vin blanc*
> *1.25 dl de vinaigre de vin blanc*
> *2 échalottes, hachées*
> *5 dl de sauce espagnole*
> *2 cuillers à soupe de cornichons hachés grossièrement*
> *1 cuiller à soupe de persil haché*
> *2 cuillers à café d'estragon haché*
> *2 cuillers à café de cerfeuil haché*

Reduce ½ cup white wine and ½ cup white wine vinegar with 2 chopped shallots to 1 tablespoon. Add 2 cups espagnole sauce and simmer 5 minutes. Just before serving, stir in 2 tablespoons coarsely chopped gherkin pickles, 1 tablespoon chopped parsley, 2 teaspoons chopped tarragon, 2 teaspoons chopped chervil, and taste for seasoning. Serve with pork, boiled beef, and broiled chicken.

Sauce Poivrade

2 tablespoons diced onion
2 tablespoons carrot
2 tablespoons celery
3 tablespoons butter or oil
1 cup white wine vinegar
1 bouquet garni
2 cups espagnole sauce or basic brown sauce
Freshly ground black pepper

50 g d'oignons
50 g de carottes
50 g de céleri
45 g de beurre ou 3 cuillers à soupe d'huile
2.5 dl de vinaigre de vin blanc
1 bouquet garni
5 dl de sauce espagnole ou de fond de veau lié
Poivre noir fraîchement moulu

Sauté 2 tablespoons each of diced onion, carrot, and celery in
3 tablespoons butter or oil. Add 1 cup white wine vinegar and a
bouquet garni and reduce to ½ cup. Add 2 cups espagnole sauce or
basic brown sauce and simmer 10-15 minutes, skimming often. Strain
the sauce and season well with freshly ground black pepper. Serve
with broiled beef. (A different sauce poivrade is often made with the
marinade from game.)

BROWN SAUCE DERIVATIVES *(continued)*
Dérivés de Sauces Brunes (suite)

Sauce Robert

½ onion, chopped
1 tablespoon butter
¾ cup white wine
¼ cup white wine vinegar
2 cups espagnole sauce or basic brown sauce
2-3 teaspoons Dijon-style mustard

> *½ oignon haché*
> *15 g de beurre*
> *2 dl de vin blanc*
> *6.5 cl de vinaigre de vin blanc*
> *5 dl de sauce espagnole ou de fond de veau lié*
> *2-3 cuillers à café de moutarde de Dijon*

This is the oldest of all sauces, dating from the Middle Ages. Sauté ½ onion, chopped, in 1 tablespoon butter until soft but not brown. Add ¾ cup white wine and ¼ cup white wine vinegar and reduce to ¼ cup. Add 2 cups espagnole sauce or basic brown sauce and bring just back to a boil. Take from the heat, stir in 2-3 teaspoons Dijon-style mustard, and taste for seasoning. Do not reboil the sauce. Serve with pork.

BECHAMEL SAUCE
Sauce Béchamel

1 cup milk
1 slice of onion, 1 small bay leaf, and
   6 peppercorns (for infusing, optional)
Salt and pepper
Pinch of grated nutmeg
For the roux:

	THIN	MEDIUM	THICK
Butter	1 tablespoon	1½ tablespoons	2 tablespoons
Flour	1 tablespoon	1½ tablespoons	2 tablespoons

Makes 1 cup sauce.

2.5 dl de lait
1 tranche d'oignon, 1 petite feuille de laurier
   et 6 grains de poivre (pour infuser, facultatif)
Sel et poivre
Une pincée de noix de muscade râpé
Pour le roux:

	FLUIDE	*MOYENNE*	*EPAISSE*
de beurre	*15 g*	*20 g*	*30 g*
de farine	*10 g*	*15 g*	*20 g*

Rendement: 2.5 dl de sauce.

Scald the milk in a saucepan. If you like, infuse it with onion, bay leaf, and peppercorns for 5-10 minutes to add flavor. Meanwhile make the roux: In a heavy based saucepan melt the butter, whisk in the flour, and cook 1-2 minutes until foaming but not browned; let it cool. Strain in the hot milk, whisk well, then bring the sauce to a boil, whisking constantly, and add salt, pepper, and nutmeg to taste. Simmer 3-5 minutes. If not used at once, rub the surface of the sauce with butter to prevent a skin forming. Béchamel can be kept 2-3 days covered in the refrigerator.

BECHAMEL SAUCE DERIVATIVES
Dérivés de Sauces Béchamel

Sauce Crème

1 cup medium béchamel sauce
¼ cup heavy cream

6.5 cl de crème fraîche
2.5 dl de sauce béchamel moyenne

Add ¼ cup heavy cream to 1 cup medium béchamel sauce and
simmer, whisking constantly, to the required consistency; taste for
seasoning. Serve with eggs, fish, vegetables, and poultry.

Cheese Sauce Mornay

1 cup thin béchamel sauce
1 egg yolk
¼ cup grated cheese (Gruyère or Parmesan)
1 tsp. Dijon mustard (optional)

2.5 dl de sauce béchamel fluide
1 jaune d'oeuf
30 g de fromage râpé
1 cuiller à café de moutarde de Dijon

Make 1 cup thin béchamel sauce. Take from the heat, beat in 1 egg
yolk and ¼ cup grated cheese and taste for seasoning. Do not reheat
the sauce or the cheese will cook into strings. Well-aged Gruyère
or Parmesan, or a mixture of both, are the best cheeses to use—the
flavor of Parmesan is somewhat sharper. The sauce can be flavored, if
you like, with 1 teaspoon Dijon mustard. For eggs, fish, poultry, white
meats, and vegetables.

Sauce Soubise

1 cup thick béchamel sauce
2 medium onions
2 tablespoons butter

2.5 dl de béchamel épaisse
2 oignons hachés
30 g de beurre

Make 1 cup thick béchamel sauce. Chop 2 medium onions, blanch them for 1 minute in boiling salted water, and drain. Melt 2 tablespoons butter in a heavy based pan; add the onions with salt and pepper. Press a piece of paper on them and cover with the lid. Cook very gently 10-15 minutes until very soft but not brown. Stir onions into sauce and work through a fine strainer. Reheat sauce and taste for seasoning. For eggs, veal, and lamb.

Method for adding a thickener. *Mains faisant la liaison.*

VELOUTE SAUCE
Le Velouté

1-1¼ cups well-flavored veal, chicken or fish stock
Salt and pepper
For the roux:
   1½ tablespoons butter
   1½ tablespoons flour

2.5-3 dl de fond de veau, de volaille ou de fumet de poisson
Sel et poivre
Pour le roux:
   20 g de beurre
   15 g de farine

Rendement: 2.5 dl de sauce velouté.

Velouté sauce can be flavored with veal, chicken, or fish and it is often made from the liquid in which food is cooked. This recipe makes 1 cup sauce.

Bring the stock to a boil. In a heavy based saucepan melt the butter, whisk in the flour, and cook 1-2 minutes until foaming but not browned. Let cool, then gradually whisk in the hot stock. Bring the sauce to a boil, whisking constantly, and add a little salt and pepper—the flavor of the sauce will be concentrated during later cooking. Simmer 5-10 minutes or longer if necessary until it is the required consistency, skimming occasionally. Taste again for seasoning.

VELOUTE SAUCE DERIVATIVES
Dérivés du Velouté

Sauce Allemande

1 cup velouté sauce (made with veal stock)
¼ cup chopped mushroom stems
1 egg yolk
Lemon juice
Grate of nutmeg

> *2.5 dl de velouté de veau*
> *30 g de queues de champignons hachées*
> *1 jaune d'oeuf*
> *Un filet de jus de citron*
> *Une pincée de noix de muscade râpé.*

To 1 cup velouté sauce made with veal stock add ¼ cup chopped mushroom stems during the simmering. Strain the sauce, and whisk in 1 egg yolk. Bring the sauce just back to a boil and season it to taste with a squeeze of lemon juice and a grate of nutmeg. Serve with veal, poultry, and vegetables.

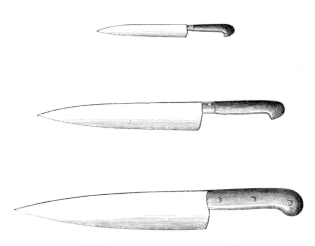

Kitchen knives. *Couteaux de cuisine.*

VELOUTE SAUCE DERIVATIVES (continued)
Dérivés du Velouté (suite)

Sauce Aurore

1 cup velouté sauce
¼ cup strained, stewed tomato pulp
   (or substitute 2 teaspoons tomato paste)
2 tablespoons butter

> *2.5 dl de velouté*
> *6.5 cl de tomates concassées (ou 2 cuillers à café de*
>   *concentré de tomate)*
> *30 g de beurre*

A short time before serving velouté sauce, whisk in ¼ cup strained stewed tomato pulp per cup of sauce. You may substitute 2 teaspoons tomato paste for the tomato pulp, but the sauce will be less delicate. Take from the heat and add 2 tablespoons butter. Serve with eggs, fish, veal, and pork.

Sauce Poulette

1 cup sauce allemande
1 tablespoon butter
2 teaspoons chopped parsley

> *2.5 dl de sauce allemande*
> *15 g de beurre*
> *2 cuillers à café de persil haché*

Just before serving sauce allemande, take from the heat and add 1 tablespoon butter and 2 teaspoons chopped parsley per cup of sauce. For calves' feet, brains, sweetbreads, and vegetables.

Sauce Suprême

¼ cup velouté sauce (made with chicken stock)
¼ cup chopped mushroom
¼ cup heavy cream
1 tablespoon butter

> *2.5 dl de velouté de volaille*
> *30 g de queues de champignons hachées*
> *6.5 cl de crème fraîche*
> *15 g de beurre*

To 1 cup velouté sauce made with chicken stock add ¼ cup chopped mushroom stems during the simmering. Strain the sauce, gradually add ¼ cup heavy cream, and simmer to the right consistency. Taste the sauce for seasoning. Take from the heat and add 1 tablespoon butter. Serve with poultry.

Sauté pan. *Plat à sauter.*

TOMATO SAUCE
Sauce Tomate

2 tablespoons butter
1 onion, chopped
2 tablespoons flour
1½ cups stock, or stock mixed with juice from canned tomatoes
2 pounds fresh tomatoes, quartered, or 3 cups (1½ pounds)
    canned tomatoes, drained and chopped
1 clove garlic, crushed
1 bouquet garni
½ teaspoon sugar
Salt and freshly ground black pepper
2 tablespoons tomato paste (optional)

Unless fresh tomatoes are ripe and glowing red, tomato sauce made with canned Italian-style tomatoes has more flavor. The recipe makes about 2½ cups sauce.

> *30 g de beurre*
> *1 oignon, haché*
> *20 g de farine*
> *3.75 dl de fond de veau, ou de fond de veau mélangé*
>   *au jus de tomates en boîte*
> *1 kg de tomates fraîches, ou 750 g de tomates en boîte,*
>   *êgouttées et hachées*
> *1 gousse d'ail écrasée*
> *1 bouquet garni*
> *½ cuiller à café de sucre*
> *Sel et poivre du moulin*
> *2 cuillers à soupe de concentré de tomate (facultatif)*
>
> *Rendement: 6 dl de sauce.*

In a saucepan melt the butter and cook the onion until soft but not brown. Stir in the flour off the heat, pour in the stock and tomato juice, if using, and bring to a boil, stirring. Add the tomatoes, garlic, bouquet garni, sugar, and salt and pepper to taste and simmer, uncovered—30-40 minutes for canned and 45-60 for fresh tomatoes, or until the tomatoes are very soft and the sauce is slightly thick.

Work the sauce through a strainer, pressing well to extract all the tomato purée, and return it to the pan. Reheat it and, if necessary, reduce it to the consistency of thin cream. If the sauce has been made from fresh tomatoes and a darker color is desired, add the tomato paste. Taste the sauce for seasoning.

Appetizers. *Hors d'oeuvre.*

HOLLANDAISE SAUCE
Sauce Hollandaise

¾ cup butter
3 tablespoons water
3 egg yolks
Salt and white pepper
Juice of ½ lemon, or to taste

Hollandaise sauce is served with poached fish, vegetables, and eggs. The recipe makes about 1 cup sauce.

180 g de beurre
3 cuillers à soupe d'eau
3 jaunes d'oeufs
Sel et poivre blanc
Le jus d'un ½ citron, ou selon goût

Rendement: 2.5 dl de sauce environ.

Melt the butter, skim froth from the surface, and let cool to tepid. In a small saucepan, whisk the water and egg yolks with a little salt and pepper for 30 seconds until light. Set the pan over low heat or in a water bath and whisk constantly until the mixture is creamy and thick enough for the whisk to leave a trail on the base of the pan. The base of the pan should never be more than hand-hot.

Take from the heat and whisk in the tepid butter, a few drops at a time. **NOTE:** Do not add the butter too fast or the sauce may curdle. When the sauce has started to thicken, the butter can be added a little faster. Do not add the milky sediment at the bottom of the butter. When all the butter is added stir in the lemon juice and taste for seasoning, adding salt, pepper, and lemon juice to taste. Hollandaise is served warm, not hot, and it should be kept warm in a water bath to avoid curdling.

If hollandaise does curdle, this is almost always because it is too hot: Take it at once from the heat and whisk in an ice cube. If this is not successful, the sauce may be started again by whisking an egg yolk and a tablespoon of water over low heat until creamy, then gradually whisking in the curdled mixture, drop by drop. However, if the sauce is badly curdled the egg yolks cook into granules and the mixture must be discarded. Very occasionally hollandaise separates through undercooking, never thickening properly. If so, try whisking in a tablespoon of boiling water. If hollandaise is too thick, add 1 tablespoon tepid water to make it lighter.

Soup tureen and accessories. *Soupière et accessoires.*

HOLLANDAISE SAUCE DERIVATIVES
Dérivés de Sauce Hollandaise

Sauce Chantilly, Mousseline or Vierge

1 cup hollandaise sauce
¼ cup heavy cream

> *2.5 dl de sauce hollandaise*
> *6.5 cl de crème fraîche fouettée*

To 1 cup hollandaise sauce, add ¼ cup heavy cream, stiffly whipped, and taste for seasoning. Serve with fish, chicken, sautéed sweetbreads, and asparagus.

Sauce Maltaise

1 cup hollandaise sauce
Juice of ½ orange
Pared rind of ½ orange

> *2.5 dl de sauce hollandaise*
> *Le jus d'un ½ orange*
> *Le zeste d' ½ orange*

To 1 cup hollandaise sauce, add the juice of ½ orange and the pared rind of ½ orange cut in needle-like shreds, blanched in boiling water for 1-2 minutes and drained. Taste for seasoning and serve particularly with asparagus.

Sauce Moutarde

1 cup hollandaise sauce
1-2 teaspoons Dijon-style mustard

2.5 dl de sauce hollandaise
1-2 cuillers à café de moutarde de Dijon

To 1 cup hollandaise sauce, add 1-2 teaspoons Dijon-style mustard or to taste. Serve with eggs and fish.

Sauce Noisette

Noisette in place of clarified butter

Beurre noisette au lieu de beurre clarifié

Use noisette instead of clarified butter to make regular hollandaise: When clarifying the butter, cook it over medium heat until nut brown. **NOTE:** Do not let it burn. Let cool and add to the egg yolk mixture as for clarified butter. Serve with eggs and vegetables.

Bearnaise Sauce
Sauce Béarnaise

¾ cup butter
3 tablespoons vinegar and 3 tablespoons white wine
10 peppercorns, crushed
3 shallots, finely chopped
1 tablespoon chopped fresh tarragon stems or tarragon leaves
    preserved in vinegar
3 egg yolks
Salt and white or cayenne pepper
1-2 tablespoons finely chopped fresh tarragon or tarragon leaves
    in vinegar (to finish)
1 tablespoon chopped chervil or parsley (to finish)

180 g de beurre
3 cuillers à soupe de vinaigre et 3 cuillers à soupe de vin blanc
10 grains de poivre
3 échalottes, finement hachées
1 cuiller à soupe de queues d'estragon frais hachées ou de feuilles
    d'estragon conservées dans du vinaigre
3 jaunes d'oeufs
Sel et poivre blanc ou de cayenne
1-2 cuillers à soupe d'estragon frais finement haché ou de feuilles
    d'estragon conservées dans du vinaigre (pour finir)
1 cuiller à soupe de cerfeuil ou de persil finement haché (pour finir)

Rendement: 2.5 dl de sauce environ.

Béarnaise is made in exactly the same way as hollandaise sauce and the same notes about keeping it warm and preventing it from curdling apply. Béarnaise is served with steak, and rich broiled or sautéed fish such as salmon; it is not worth making if only dried tarragon is available. Makes about 1 cup sauce.

Melt the butter, skim any scum from the surface, and let cool to tepid. In a small saucepan boil the vinegar with the peppercorns, chopped shallots, and 1 tablespoon tarragon stems or leaves until reduced to 2 tablespoons. Let cool, add the egg yolks, a little salt and pepper, and whisk for 30 seconds until light. Set the pan over low heat or in a water bath and whisk constantly until the mixture is creamy and quite thick—thicker than for hollandaise. The base of the pan should never be more than hand-hot. Take from the heat and whisk in the tepid butter, a few drops at a time. When the sauce has thickened, the butter can be added faster. Do not add the milky sediment at the bottom of the butter.

When all the butter is added, strain the sauce, pressing well to extract all the mixture. Add the chopped tarragon and the chervil or parsley and taste for seasoning. Béarnaise should be quite piquant with pepper.

Bearnaise Sauce Derivatives
Dérivés de Sauce Béarnaise

Sauce Choron

1 cup béarnaise sauce
1½ tablespoons tomato paste

2.5 dl de sauce béarnaise
1½ cuillers à soupe de concentré de tomate

To 1 cup béarnaise sauce, add 1½ tablespoons tomato paste.
Serve with steak, fish, and eggs.

Sauce Foyot

1 cup béarnaise sauce
1 teaspoon meat glaze

2.5 dl de sauce béarnaise
1 cuiller à café de glace de viande

To 1 cup béarnaise sauce, add 1 teaspoon meat glaze. The sauce
should be the color of café au lait. Serve with steak.

Green Peppercorn Béarnaise
Béarnaise au Poivre Vert

1 cup béarnaise sauce
1 tablespoon drained, crushed green peppercorns

2.5 dl de sauce béarnaise
1 cuiller à soupe de grains de poivre vert égouttés et pilés au lieu de feuilles d'estragon et de cerfeuil hachées

Omit the chopped tarragon and chervil leaves added at the end of béarnaise sauce and add 1 tablespoon drained and crushed green peppercorns to every cup of sauce. (Green peppercorns preserved in vinegar are obtainable at specialty stores; once opened they can be kept in their liquid, tightly covered in the refrigerator, for 1-2 months). Serve with steak and salmon.

Set of pans in a water bath. *Caisse à bain-marie.*

WHITE BUTTER SAUCE
Sauce Beurre Blanc

3 tablespoons white wine vinegar
3 tablespoons dry white wine
2 shallots, very finely chopped
1 cup butter, very cold
Salt and white pepper

> *3 cuillers à soupe de vinaigre de vin blanc*
> *3 cuillers à soupe de vin blanc sec*
> *2 échalottes, très finement hachées*
> *250 g de beurre, très froid*
> *Sel et poivre blanc*

White butter sauce comes from the Loire Valley. It is traditionally made with the local Sancerre wine and served with pike from the river. It resembles hollandaise and béarnaise sauces, but is even more delicate as it is made simply of butter whisked into a reduction of wine, vinegar, and shallots. The butter must be at exactly the right temperature to achieve a smooth, creamy sauce. The recipe makes 1 cup sauce.

In a small saucepan (not aluminum), boil the wine vinegar, wine, and shallots until reduced to 1 tablespoon. Set the pan over low heat and whisk in the butter gradually, in small pieces, to make a smooth, creamy sauce. Work sometimes over low heat and sometimes off the heat, so that the butter softens and thickens the sauce without melting. Season to taste with salt and white pepper and serve as soon as possible—if kept warm, it easily melts and becomes oily. If it must be kept warm for a few minutes, keep it over warm—but not boiling—water.

WHITE WINE BUTTER SAUCE
Sauce Vin Blanc au Beurre

2 shallots, finely chopped
1 cup butter
⅓ cup white wine
1 tablespoon heavy cream
Juice of ¼ lemon
½ teaspoon fish glaze
Salt and pepper

> *2 échalottes, finement hachées*
> *250 g de beurre*
> *1 dl de vin blanc*
> *1 cuiller à soupe de crème fraîche*
> *Le jus d'un ¼ de citron*
> *½ cuiller à café de glace de poisson*
> *Sel et poivre*

In a small saucepan (not aluminum), sauté the shallots in 1 tablespoon of the butter, stirring constantly. **NOTE:** Do not allow them to brown. Add the wine and cook about 5 minutes or until reduced to 1-2 tablespoons. **NOTE:** The mixture will be very thick and of a syrupy consistency. Add the cream and reduce again, to about 1-2 tablespoons. Set the pan over low heat and whisk in the rest of the butter gradually, in small pieces, to make a smooth creamy sauce. Work sometimes over low heat and sometimes off the heat, so that the butter softens and thickens the sauce without melting. Whisk in the lemon juice and fish glaze and season to taste with salt and pepper. The sauce can be kept warm over warm—but not boiling—water but is best served immediately. Serve with fish.

MAYONNAISE
Mayonnaise

2 egg yolks
Salt and white pepper
2 tablespoons white wine vinegar or 1 tablespoon lemon juice or to taste
Dry mustard or Dijon-style mustard (optional)
1½ cups oil

Makes about 1½ cups mayonnaise.

> *2 jaunes d'oeufs*
> *Sel et poivre blanc*
> *2 cuillers à soupe de vinaigre de vin blanc ou 1 cuiller à soupe*
> *de jus de citron ou selon goût*
> *Moutarde en poudre ou moutarde de Dijon (facultatif)*
> *3.75-4 dl d'huile*
>
> *Rendement: 4 dl de mayonnaise environ.*

All the ingredients for mayonnaise must be at room temperature. If the yolks are too cold the mayonnaise will not emulsify. If the oil is too cool, heat the bowl or the oil just to tepid. On a cold day, warm the bowl and whisk in hot water before beginning.

Beat the egg yolks with a little salt, pepper, 1 tablespoon of vinegar (or lemon juice), and mustard, if using, until thick, in a small bowl with a whisk or with an electric beater. Add the oil, drop by drop, whisking constantly. **NOTE:** If oil is added too quickly the mayonnaise will curdle. When 2 tablespoons of oil have been added, the mixture should be very thick. The remaining oil can be added a little more quickly, either 1 tablespoon at a time and beaten thoroughly between each addition until it is absorbed or in a thin steady stream if using an electric mixer.

When all the oil has been added, stir in the remaining vinegar or lemon juice to taste, more mustard (if used), and salt and white pepper as needed. The amount of seasoning depends very much on the oil and vinegar used and what the mayonnaise is to accompany. Thin the mayonnaise, if necessary, with a little warm water.

Mayonnaise is best stored in a covered container at room temperature, but if it is kept in the refrigerator, it should be brought to room temperature before stirring; otherwise it may curdle. It can be kept 2-3 days.

If mayonnaise does curdle during making or on standing: Beat in a tablespoon of boiling water. If it does not reemulsify, start again beating a fresh egg yolk with salt and pepper, then whisking in the curdled mixture drop by drop. Alternatively, if the mayonnaise is to be flavored with mustard, the curdled mixture can be gradually beaten into a teaspoonful of Dijon-style mustard.

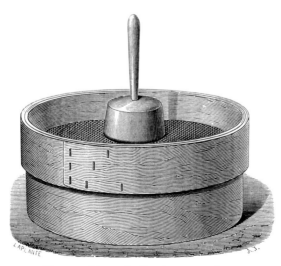

Sieve used to purée. *Tamis pour purée.*

MAYONNAISE DERIVATIVES
Dérivés de Mayonnaise

Mayonnaise Chantilly

1 cup mayonnaise
¼ cup heavy cream

2.5 dl de mayonnaise
6.5 cl de crème fraîche, fouettée

To 1 cup mayonnaise add ¼ cup heavy cream, stiffly whipped, and taste for seasoning. Serve with vegetable salads and asparagus.

Firm Mayonnaise
Mayonnaise Collée

½ envelope gelatin
¼ cup aspic or consommé
1 cup mayonnaise

4 g de gelatine
6.5 cl de gelée ou de consommé
2.5 dl de mayonnaise

Firm mayonnaise is set with gelatin so it will hold shape when used for coating chaudfroids of fish, poultry, and eggs; it can be substituted for chaudfroid sauce based on velouté. Sprinkle ½ envelope gelatin over ¼ cup aspic or consommé in a small pan and let stand 5 minutes until soft. Dissolve over a pan of hot water and stir into 1 cup mayonnaise. Let cool until on the point of setting and use like chaudfroid sauce.

Green Mayonnaise
Mayonnaise Verte

2 cups boiling water
6-8 spinach leaves without stems
¼ cup watercress leaves
¼ cup parsley sprigs
2 tablespoons tarragon or chervil leaves
1 cup of mayonnaise

> *5 dl d'eau bouillante (pour blanchir)*
> *6-8 feuilles d'épinards sans tiges*
> *10 g de feuilles de cresson*
> *10 g de feuilles de persil*
> *2 cuillers à soupe de feuilles d'estragon ou de cerfeuil*
> *2.5 dl de mayonnaise*

In about 2 cups boiling water blanch 6-8 spinach leaves without stems, ¼ cup watercress leaves, ¼ cup parsley sprigs, and 2 tablespoons tarragon or chervil leaves. Drain thoroughly, refresh with cold water, and squeeze in a towel to obtain a green liquid. Into 1 cup of mayonnaise stir 2 tablespoons of this liquid, or enough to color the mayonnaise a pale green. Taste for seasoning and serve with fish, eggs, and vegetables.

Pan for glazing. *Casserole à glacer.*

MAYONNAISE DERIVATIVES *(continued)*
Dérivés de Mayonnaise (suite)

Sauce Remoulade

1 cup mayonnaise
1 tsp Dijon mustard
2 tablespoons chopped capers
3 tablespoons chopped gherkin pickles
1 tablespoon chopped parsley
2 teaspoons chopped chervil
2 teaspoons chopped tarragon
½ teaspoon anchovy essence or 1 teaspoon crushed anchovy fillets

2.5 dl de mayonnaise
1 cuiller à café de moutarde de Dijon
2 cuillers à soupe de câpres hachées
3 cuillers à soupe de cornichons hachés
1 cuiller à soupe de persil haché
2 cuillers à café de cerfeuil haché
2 cuillers à café d'estragon haché
½ cuiller à café d'essence d'anchois ou 1 cuiller à café
   de filets d'anchois pilés

To 1 cup mayonnaise add 1 teaspoon Dijon-style mustard,
2 tablespoons chopped capers, 3 tablespoons chopped gherkin
pickles, 1 tablespoon chopped parsley, 2 teaspoons chopped chervil,
2 teaspoons chopped tarragon, and ½ teaspoon anchovy essence
or 1 teaspoon crushed anchovy fillets. Mix well, taste for seasoning,
and serve with eggs and hot fried fish.

STEWED TOMATO PULP
Tomates Concassées

2 tablespoons oil
½ shallot or ½ onion, finely chopped
2 pounds fresh tomatoes, peeled, seeded and chopped
1 small bouquet garni
Salt and pepper

Makes about 2 cups stewed tomato pulp.

> *2 cuillers à soupe d'huile*
> *½ échalotte ou ½ petit oignon, finement haché*
> *1 kg de tomates fraîches, mondées, épépinées et concassées*
> *1 petit bouquet garni*
> *Sel et poivre*
>
> *Rendement: 5 dl de tomates concassées.*

Heat the oil, add the chopped shallot or onion and sauté gently, stirring often, for about 3-5 minutes or until soft but not brown. Add the tomatoes, bouquet garni, salt and pepper, and cook over medium heat, stirring frequently, for 20-30 minutes or until nearly all the moisture has evaporated. Taste for seasoning.

CHAPTER 3

PASTRIES AND CAKES

Les Pâtes et les Gâteaux

Simple pastry dough (*Pâte Brisée*) in the
La Varenne kitchen is the foundation of
savory open tarts, quiches, and double crust
tourtes. The sweet version (*Pâte Sucrée*) is
the container for innumerable fruits and other
sweet tarts. Two other important doughs are
Puff Pastry, with its many layers and generous
proportion of butter, and Choux Pastry with
a high egg content so the dough rises in the
oven to form crisp cream puffs. Choux
can also be deep fried as *beignets*.

Two kinds of cake batter dominate French
pastry shops: *Génoise* which is a sponge made
with whole eggs, and drier *Biscuit* in which the
eggs are separated. Brioche dough relies on
yeast to raise it and give flavor.

PIE PASTRY
Pâte Brisée

Pie Shell ◄ OR ► Tartlets	7-8 INCH	9-10 INCH	11-12 INCH
	5	7	8
flour	1 cup	1½ cups	2 cups
unsalted butter	¼ cup	⅓ cup	½ cup
egg yolk	1	1	2
salt	⅓ tsp.	¾ tsp.	1 tsp.
cold water	3½-4 T.	4½-5 T.	5½-6 T.

Une Croustade ◄ *OU* ► *Tartelettes*	*18-20 CM DE DIAMÈTRE*	*24-26 CM DE DIAMÈTRE*	*28-30 CM DE DIAMÈTRE*
	5	*7*	*8*
de farine	*125 g*	*200 g*	*250 g*
de beurre	*60 g*	*100 g*	*125 g*
jaunes d'oeuf	*1*	*1*	*2*
de sel	*2 g*	*4 g*	*5 g*
cuillers à soupe d'eau froide	*1½-2*	*2½-3*	*3½-4*

Sift flour onto a marble slab or board and make a large well in the center. Pound butter to soften slightly. Place butter, egg yolks, salt, and smaller amount of water in the well and work together with the fingertips of one hand until partly mixed. Gradually work in flour, pulling dough into large crumbs using the fingertips of both hands. If the crumbs are dry, sprinkle over a tablespoon more water. Press dough firmly together—it should be soft but not sticky. Work on a lightly floured marble or board, pushing dough away with the heel of the hand and gathering it up with a dough scraper until smooth and pliable. Press dough into a ball, wrap in parchment paper, foil, plastic wrap, or a plastic bag, and chill 30 minutes. It can be stored, tightly wrapped, in the refrigerator for up to 3 days.

Vanilla bavarian cream. *Bavarois à la vanille.*

SWEET PIE PASTRY
Pâte Sucrée

Pie Shell	7-8 INCH	9-10 INCH	11-12 INCH
◄ OR ►			
Tartlets	5	7	8
flour	1 cup	1½ cups	1¾ cups
salt	¼ tsp.	¼ tsp.	½ tsp.
sugar	¼ cup	⅓ cup	½ cup
egg yolks	2	3	4
vanilla extract	½ tsp.	½ tsp.	1 tsp.
unsalted butter	¼ cup	⅓ cup	½ cup

Une Croustade	*18-20 CM DE DIAMÈTRE*	*24-26 CM DE DIAMÈTRE*	*28-30 CM DE DIAMÈTRE*
◄ *OU* ►			
Tartelettes	*5*	*7*	*8*
de farine	*125 g*	*200 g*	*250 g*
de sel	*1 g*	*1 g*	*2 g*
de sucre	*50 g*	*80 g*	*100 g*
jaunes d'oeufs	*2*	*3*	*4*
cuiller à café de vanille	*½*	*½*	*1*
de beurre	*60 g*	*100 g*	*125 g*

Sift the flour onto a marble slab or board and make a large well in the center. Put the salt, sugar, egg yolks, and vanilla extract in the well and mix them with your fingers until the sugar dissolves. Pound on the butter to soften it slightly, add it to the well, and quickly work it with the other ingredients using the fingertips of one hand until partly mixed. Gradually work in the flour, pulling the dough into large crumbs using the fingertips of both hands. Mix the dough with a cutting motion, using a dough scraper. When the dough is smooth, work it on a lightly floured marble slab or board, pushing it away with the heel of the hand and gathering it up with the dough scraper until it is pliable and peels away easily in one piece. Press the dough into a ball. Wrap it in parchment paper, foil, plastic wrap or a plastic bag, and chill 30 minutes. The dough can be stored, tightly wrapped, in the refrigerator for up to 3 days.

Copper jam pan. *Bassine à confiture en cuivre.*

CHOUX PASTRY
Pâte à Choux

3-inch Cream Puffs (ABOUT 1½ INCHES BEFORE BAKING)	15	20	25
flour	½ cup	⅔ cup	1 cup
water	½ cup	⅔ cup	1 cup
salt	⅓ tsp.	½ tsp.	¾ tsp.
unsalted butter	¼ cup	⅓ cup	½ cup
eggs	2 large	3-4	4-5

When making choux pastry with ½ cup flour, ingredients must be measured extremely accurately.

Choux de 7 cm de Diamètre (ENVIRON 3-4 CM DE DIAMÈTRE AVANT LA CUISSON)	15	20	25
de farine	75 g	110 g	150 g
d'eau	1.25 dl	1.85 dl	2.5 dl
de sel	2 g	3 g	4 g
de beurre	50 g	75 g	100 g
oeufs	2	3	4

Sift the flour onto a piece of wax paper. In a saucepan, heat the water, salt, and butter until the butter is melted, then bring to a boil and take from the heat. **NOTE:** Prolonged boiling evaporates the water and changes the proportions of the dough. As soon as the pan is taken from the heat add all the flour at once and beat vigorously with a wooden spatula for a few seconds until the mixture is smooth and pulls away from the pan to form a ball. Beat ½-1 minute over low heat to dry the mixture.

Set aside one egg and beat it in a bowl. With a wooden spatula beat the remaining eggs into the dough, one by one, beating thoroughly after each addition. Beat enough of the reserved egg into the dough to make a mixture that is very shiny and just falls from the spoon. **NOTE:** All reserved egg may not be needed; if too much is added, the dough cannot be shaped.

Choux pastry can be stored up to 8 hours. Rub the surface with butter while the dough is still warm. When cool, cover tightly and store in the refrigerator. However, the dough puffs better if used immediately.

Mortar and pestle. *Mortier et pilon.*

PUFF PASTRY
Pâte Feuilletée

Vol-au-vent	8 INCH	9 INCH	10-11 INCH
◄ OR ►			
3-inch Bouchées	9-10	13-15	18-20
unsalted butter	⅔-1 cup	1¼-1½ cups	1½-2 cups
flour	2 cups	3 cups	4 cups
salt	1 tsp.	1-½ tsp.	2 tsp.
lemon juice (optional)	1 tsp.	1-½ tsp.	2 tsp.
ice water	½-⅔ cup	¾-1 cup	1¼-1⅓ cups

Un Vol-au-vent	*20 CM DE DIAMÈTRE*	*22 CM DE DIAMÈTRE*	*25-27 CM DE DIAMÈTRE*
◄ *OU* ►			
Bouchées de 7 cm de Diamètre	*9-10*	*13-15*	*18-20*
de beurre	*200-250 g*	*300-375 g*	*400-500 g*
de farine	*250 g*	*375 g*	*500 g*
de sel	*5 g*	*7 g*	*10 g*
cuillers à café de jus de citron (facultatif)	*1*	*1½*	*2*
environ d'eau glacée	*1.3-1.5 dl*	*1.8-2 dl*	*2.75-3 dl*
de beurre	*60 g*	*100 g*	*125 g*

For puff pastry it is important to work on a cold surface. If your working surface is warm, chill it by placing ice trays on top before making the détrempe and before every 2 turns. Dry the working surface well after removing the ice.

Melt or soften 1 tablespoon of the butter. Keep the rest of the butter cold. Sift the flour onto a cold marble slab or board, make a well in the center, add the salt, lemon juice, the smaller amount of water, and the 1 tablespoon of butter. Work together with the fingertips until well mixed, then gradually work in the flour, pulling the dough into large crumbs using the fingertips of both hands. If the crumbs are dry, add more water—the amount of water needed depends very much on the type of flour used. Cut the dough several times with a dough scraper to ensure that the ingredients are evenly blended but do not knead it. Press the dough to form a ball. It should be quite soft. This dough is called the détrempe. Wrap it in parchment paper, plastic wrap or a plastic bag and chill 15 minutes.

The amount of butter used depends on the desired richness of the dough and on your experience. The usual practice is to use half the weight of the détrempe in butter, but you may use up to the maximum indicated in the recipe. Lightly flour the butter, put between two sheets of wax paper and flatten it with the rolling pin. Fold it, replace between the paper and continue pounding and folding it until pliable but not sticky—the butter should be the same consistency as the détrempe. Shape it into a 6-inch square and flour it lightly. Roll out the dough on a floured marble slab or board to a 12-inch square, thicker in the center than at the sides. Set the butter in the center and fold the dough around it like an envelope.

Making sure your working surface is well floured, place the package of dough seams down and bring the rolling pin down on the dough 3-4 times to flatten it slightly. Roll it out to a rectangle 7-8 inches wide and 18-20 inches long. Fold the rectangle of dough into three,

PUFF PASTRY *(continued)*
Pâte Feuilletée (suite)

one end inside, as in folding a business letter, with the layers as accurate as possible. Seal the edges with the rolling pin and turn the dough a quarter turn (90°) to bring the closed seam to your left side so the dough opens like a book. This is called a turn. Roll out again and fold in three. This is the second turn. Keep a note of these turns by marking the dough lightly with the appropriate number of fingerprints. Wrap the dough and chill 15 minutes.

Repeat the rolling process, giving the dough 6 turns altogether with a 15 minute rest in the refrigerator between every two turns. Chill at least 15 minutes before using.

Puff pastry that has had either 4 or 6 turns can be kept, tightly wrapped, in the refrigerator for up to a week or for up to 3 months in the freezer. If keeping it after 4 turns, do the last 2 turns just before shaping.

King's cake. *Galette des rois.*

GENOISE
Génoise

	4 SERVINGS	6 SERVINGS
flour	½ cup	¾ cup
salt	pinch	pinch
butter (optional)	3 T.	4 T.
eggs	3	4
sugar	½ cup	⅔ cup
flavoring	½ teaspoon vanilla, or grated rind 1 lemon or 1 orange, or 1 teaspoon orange flower water, or 2-3 drops anise oil	

Génoise batter made with 3 eggs should be baked in an 8-9 inch layer pan or a 7-8 inch springform pan, making a cake to serve 4 people. A 4-egg génoise is baked in a 9-10 inch layer pan or an 8-inch springform pan and serves 6. For a lighter, somewhat drier cake, cake flour may be substituted for all-purpose flour.

	4 PERSONNES	*6 PERSONNES*
de farine	*90 g*	*125 g*
de sel	*pincée*	*pincée*
de beurre (facultatif)	*45 g*	*60 g*
oeufs	*3*	*4*
de sucre	*90 g*	*125 g*
pour parfumer	*½ cuiller à café de vanille* *ou le zeste râpé d'un citron ou d'une orange* *ou 1 cuiller à café d'eau de fleur d'oranger* *ou 2-3 gouttes d'huile d'anis*	

L'appareil à génoise fait avec 3 oeufs est cuit dans un moule à manqué de 20-22 cm de diamètre et sert 4 personnes. L'appareil à 4 oeufs fait un gâteau de 23-25 cm de diamètre pour 6 personnes. Four modéré (175°C; n° 4).

GENOISE *(continued)*
Génoise *(suite)*

Brush the cake pan with melted butter. If you like, line the base with a circle of wax paper that fits exactly and butter it also. Leave for a few minutes and then sprinkle the pan with flour, discarding the excess. Set the oven at moderate (350°F). Sift the flour with the salt 2-3 times. Clarify the butter.

Put the eggs in a large bowl, preferably copper, and gradually beat in the sugar. Set the bowl over a pan of hot but not boiling water or over very low heat and beat 8-10 minutes or until the mixture is light and thick enough to leave a ribbon trail when the whisk is lifted. Take the bowl from the heat, add the chosen flavoring, and continue beating until the mixture is cool.

Sift the flour over the batter in three batches, folding in each batch with a wooden spatula or metal spoon as lightly as possible. Just after the last batch, add the butter and fold in both together. **NOTE:** The batter quickly loses volume after the butter is added.

Pour the batter into the prepared cake pan and bake in the heated oven, allowing 25-30 minutes for a small cake or 35-40 minutes for a larger one, or until the cake shrinks slightly from the sides of the pan and the top springs back when lightly pressed with a fingertip. Run a knife around the sides of the cake to loosen it and turn out on a rack to cool.

A génoise can be kept for several days in an airtight container or it can be frozen.

SPONGE CAKE
Biscuit

	4 SERVINGS	6 SERVINGS
flour	½ cup	¾ cup
salt	pinch	pinch
eggs, separated	3	4
sugar	½ cup	¾ cup
flavoring	½ teaspoon vanilla or grated rind 1 lemon or 1 orange or 1 teaspoon orange flower water or 2-3 drops anise oil	

Sponge cake batter made with 3 eggs should be baked in an 8-9 inch layer pan or a 7-8 inch springform pan, making a cake to serve 4 people. A 4-egg sponge is baked in a 9-10 inch layer pan or an 8-inch springform pan and serves 6.

	4 PERSONNES	6 PERSONNES
de farine	*90 g*	*120 g*
de sel	*pincée*	*pincée*
oeufs, clarifiés	*3*	*4*
de sucre	*130 g*	*180 g*
pour parfumer	*½ cuiller à café de vanille ou le zeste râpé d'un citron ou d'une orange ou 1 cuiller à café d'eau de fleur d'oranger ou 2-3 gouttes d'huile d'anis*	

L'appareil à biscuit fait avec 3 oeufs est cuit dans un moule à manqué de 20-22 cm de diamètre et sert 4 personnes. L'appareil à 4 oeufs fait un gâteau de 23-25 cm de diamètre pour 6 personnes. Four modéré (175° C; n° 4).

SPONGE CAKE *(continued)*
Biscuit (suite)

Thoroughly brush the cake pan with melted butter. If you like, line
the base with a circle of wax paper that fits exactly, and butter it
also. Leave for a few minutes and then sprinkle the pan with flour,
discarding the excess. Set oven at moderate (350°F). Sift the flour
with the salt.

Beat the egg yolks with half the sugar and the flavoring until thick
and light and the mixture leaves a thick ribbon trail when the whisk is
lifted. Stiffly whip the egg whites, if possible using a copper bowl. Add
the rest of the sugar and beat 20-30 seconds longer or until glossy.
As lightly as possible, fold the flour and egg whites into the egg yolk
mixture in 2-3 batches, using a wooden spatula or metal spoon.

Pour the batter into the prepared pan and bake in the heated oven,
allowing 25-30 minutes for a small cake, or 35-40 minutes for a large
one, or until the cake shrinks slightly from the sides of the pan and
the top springs back when lightly pressed with a fingertip. Run a
knife around the sides of the cake to loosen it and turn out on a
rack to cool.

The cake is best served fresh but it can be kept a day or two in an
airtight container. It freezes well.

BRIOCHE
Brioche

4 cups flour
2½ teaspoons salt
2 tablespoons sugar
1 package dry yeast or 1 cake compressed yeast
2 tablespoons lukewarm water
6 eggs
1 cup unsalted butter

Makes 15 small brioches or 2 large 6-inch loaves.

500 g de farine
12 g de sel
30 g de sucre
15 g de levure
2 cuillers à soupe d'eau tiède
6 oeufs
250 g de beurre

Rendement: 15 petites brioches ou 2 grosses brioches
(moules de 21 cm).

BRIOCHE *(continued)*
Brioche (suite)

Sift the flour onto a marble slab or board and make a very large well in the center. Place the salt and the sugar in little piles on one side of the well, and the crumbled yeast on another side of the well, as far from the salt and sugar as possible. Using your fingers, dilute the yeast with the lukewarm water, without mixing in the salt or sugar. Mix about ⅛ of the flour into the yeast, still keeping the mixture on one side of the flour well. Leave to rise for about 5-10 minutes. Break in 5 of the eggs. With your fingertips mix the eggs with the salt, sugar, and yeast mixture briefly together; still using your fingertips, flick some of the flour over the center mixture so the center is no longer visible. Quickly draw in the rest of the flour with both hands, being careful not to let the liquid escape outside the well. Pull the dough into large crumbs using the fingertips of both hands. If it is dry beat the last egg and add it. Press the dough firmly together—it should be soft and sticky.

Mix the dough by pinching off 2 small portions between the thumb and forefinger of each hand and placing the portions removed on the other end of the mass of dough. Repeat this pinching motion about 5-7 times. Now knead the dough by lifting it up and slapping it down on a floured board or marble slab for 5-10 minutes or until it is very smooth and elastic.

Pound on the butter to soften it thoroughly. Place the block of softened butter on the dough, and mix it in with the same pinching motion used above. After 5-7 times, knead the dough by slapping it on the board as lightly as possible, just until the butter is completely mixed in.

Transfer the dough to a lightly oiled bowl, turn it over, cover the bowl with a damp cloth, and let it rise at room temperature for about 2 hours or until doubled in bulk. Remove to a floured board or marble slab and fold in three, patting it to knock out the air. Cover with a damp cloth and leave to rise again until doubled at room temperature or overnight in the refrigerator. Brioche dough is much easier to handle if chilled in the refrigerator.

NOTE: Up to 2 packages or 30 g of yeast can be used if the dough must rise as quickly as possible.

Soft boiled eggs. *Oeufs à la coque.*

CREPES
Crêpes

Crêpes
(6-7 INCHES IN DIAMETER)

	18	28
flour	1 cup	1½ cups
salt	⅓ tsp.	¾ tsp.
milk	1 cup	1½ cups
eggs	3 large	4 large
melted butter or oil	2 T.	3 T.
clarified butter or oil (for frying)	⅓ cup	½ cup

Crêpes
(15-18 CM DE DIAMÈTRE)

	18	*28*
de farine	*125 g*	*200 g*
de sel	*2 g*	*4 g*
de lait	*2.5 dl*	*3.75 dl*
oeufs	*3*	*4*
cuillers à soupe de beurre fondu ou d'huile	*2*	*3*
de beurre clarifié ou d'huile (pour la cuisson des crêpes)	*100 g*	*125 g*

Sift the flour into a bowl, make a well in the center, and add the salt and half the milk. Gradually whisk in the flour to make a smooth batter. Whisk in the eggs. **NOTE:** Do not beat the batter too much or it will become elastic and the finished crêpes will be tough. Stir in the melted butter or oil with half the remaining milk, cover, and let the batter stand 1-2 hours. It will thicken slightly as the grains of starch in the flour expand. The batter can be kept up to 24 hours in the refrigerator.

Just before using: Stir in enough of the remaining milk to make a batter the consistency of thin cream. Brush or rub the crêpe pan with butter or oil and heat until very hot (a drop of batter will sizzle at once). Add 2-3 tablespoons batter to the hot pan, turning it quickly so the bottom is evenly coated. Cook over fairly high heat until browned, then toss the crêpe or turn with a spatula. Cook for 10 seconds to brown the other side and turn out onto a plate. Continue cooking the remaining crêpes in the same way, greasing the pan only when the crêpes start to stick.

As the crêpes are cooked, pile them one on the top of the other to keep the bottom ones moist and warm. Crêpes can be made ahead, layered with wax paper and stored in a plastic bag. They can be kept in the refrigerator for up to 3 days or for 2-3 months in the freezer.

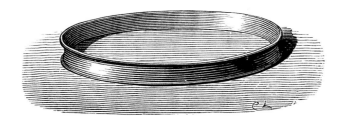

Flan ring. *Moule à flan.*

CHAPTER 4

FILLINGS, FROSTINGS, AND MERINGUES

Les Crèmes, Glaçages et les Meringues

A French cake is rarely complete without
an icing, and very often a filling as well.
The pastry chefs at La Varenne display an
astonishing versatility with butter cream,
which is often used for coating as well as
filling a cake. For coating, the trio of Fondant,
Royal, and Glacé icings add further options.
Meringue made with just two ingredients,
sugar and egg whites, has a multitude of uses
in the pastry kitchen. Of the three types,
Swiss Meringue is lightest but does not hold
up well, Italian Meringue is firmer and can be
kept for several days, while Cooked Meringue
is the stiffest and most intense of all.

CHANTILLY CREAM
Crème Chantilly

1 cup heavy cream or crème fraîche
1 tablespoon sugar
½ teaspoon vanilla

Makes about 2 cups whipped cream.

> *2.5 dl de crème fleurette; ou 2 dl de crème fraîche et 5 cl de lait*
> *1 cuiller à soupe de sucre*
> *½ cuiller à café de vanille*
>
> *Rendement: 5 dl de crème chantilly environ.*

Chill the cream, bowl, and whisk before whipping.

Whip the cream until it starts to thicken. Add the sugar and vanilla and continue beating until the cream holds a shape and sticks to the whisk. Be careful not to overbeat, which will cause the cream to turn to butter. **NOTE:** If using crème fraîche to make Chantilly cream, a small amount of milk should be added to the cream before beating to lighten it.

Copper pan for boiling sugar. *Poêlon à sucre en cuivre.*

CREME FRAICHE
Crème Fraîche

1 pint (2 cups) heavy cream
½ pint (1 cup) buttermilk, sour cream or yogurt

> *5 dl de crème fleurette*
> *2.5 dl de crème aigre ou de yaourt*

Stir together the heavy cream and the buttermilk, sour cream or yogurt in a saucepan. Heat gently until the mixture is no longer cold, around body temperature. Pour into a container and partially cover. Leave at room temperature for 6-8 hours or overnight, or until the cream is thickened and slightly acidic in taste. **NOTE:** On a hot day, the cream may thicken faster; on a cold day, it will take longer. Stir the cream, cover and refrigerate.

When making a new batch of crème fraîche, you may use ½ pint of the crème fraîche you have made instead of the buttermilk in the recipe.

NOTE: Crème fraîche tastes best if made with buttermilk, next best with sour cream and last with yogurt. It keeps longest if made with yogurt, next with buttermilk and shortest if made with sour cream.

BUTTER CREAM FROSTING
Crème au Beurre

Most butter creams (except those containing fruit purée) can be kept in the refrigerator for up to a week or can be frozen. However, chocolate butter cream becomes too stiff to work if it is chilled and must be softened by pushing through a sieve or by being warmed and thoroughly beaten. Butter creams containing fruit purée or a liquid such as a liqueur tend to separate when cold; if warmed and thoroughly beaten, they will regain their smoothness. Butter cream made with Italian meringue, which is lighter both in color and consistency than butter cream made with egg yolks, is used for light-colored or delicate cakes.

Apple charlotte. *Charlotte aux pommes.*

EGG YOLK BUTTER CREAM FROSTING
Crème au Beurre aux Jaunes d'Oeufs

	1½ CUPS FROSTING	2 CUPS FROSTING
egg yolks	3	4
sugar	7 T.	9 T.
water	¼ cup	⅓ cup
unsalted butter	¾ cup	1 cup
chosen flavoring (see below)		

	3.5 DL DE CRÈME ENVIRON	*5 DL DE CRÈME ENVIRON*
jaunes d'oeufs	*3*	*4*
de sucre	*90 g*	*120 g*
d'eau	*6.5 cl*	*1 dl*
de beurre	*200 g*	*250 g*
parfum au choix (voir ci-dessous)		

In a bowl beat the egg yolks lightly until mixed. Heat the sugar with the water until dissolved, bring to a boil and boil until the syrup reaches the soft ball stage (239°F/115°C on a sugar thermometer). Gradually pour the hot sugar syrup onto the egg yolks, beating constantly, and continue beating until the mixture is cool and thick. Cream the butter and gradually beat it into the egg mixture. Beat in the flavoring.

ITALIAN MERINGUE BUTTER CREAM FROSTING
Crème au Beurre à la Meringue Italienne

	3 CUPS FROSTING	4 CUPS FROSTING
sugar	⅚ cup	1¼ cups
water	⅓ cup	½ cup
egg whites	3	4
unsalted butter	1¼ cups	1⅔ cups
chosen flavoring (see below)		

	7.5 DL DE CRÈME ENVIRON	*1 LITRE DE CRÈME ENVIRON*
de sucre	*180 g*	*240 g*
d'eau	*1 dl*	*1.25 dl*
blancs d'oeufs	*3*	*4*
de beurre	*300 g*	*400 g*
parfum au choix (voir ci-dessous)		

Make the Italian meringue and whisk it until cool. Thoroughly cream the butter and whisk in the meringue, a little at a time. Beat in the flavoring.

FLAVORINGS *for* BUTTER CREAM FROSTING
Parfums pour la Crème au Beurre

Chocolate
Chocolat

1 cup butter cream frosting
3 squares (3 oz.) semisweet chocolate

2.5 dl de crème au beurre
100 g de chocolat à croquer fondu

To every cup of frosting add 3 squares (3 oz) semisweet chocolate, chopped, melted over hot water, and left until cool.

Coffee
Café

1 cup butter cream frosting
2-3 teaspoons dry instant coffee
1 cup hot water

2.5 dl de crème au beurre
2 cuillers à café de café soluble, dissout dans
1 cuiller à soupe d'eau chaude

To every cup of frosting add 2-3 teaspoons dry instant coffee dissolved in 1 tablespoon hot water.

FLAVORINGS *for* BUTTER CREAM FROSTING *(continued)*
Parfums pour la Crème au Beurre (suite)

Lemon or Orange
Citron ou Orange

1 cup butter cream frosting
Zest of 2 lemons or 1 orange, finely grated
1 tablespoon orange liqueur such as Grand Marnier

> *2.5 dl de crème au beurre*
> *Le zeste finement râpé de 2 citrons ou 1 orange*
> *Crème au beurre à l'orange: 1 cuiller à soupe de liqueur à l'orange tel que Grand Marnier*

To every cup of butter cream beat the finely grated rind of 2 lemons or 1 orange. To orange butter cream add 1 tablespoon orange liqueur such as Grand Marnier.

Praline
Praliné

1 cup butter cream frosting
5 tablespoons almonds
3 tablespoons sugar

> *2.5 dl de crème au beurre*
> *40 g d'amandes*
> *40 g de sucre*

In a small pan heat equal weights of blanched or unblanched almonds and granulated sugar, allowing 5 tablespoons of almonds, and 3 tablespoons sugar for every cup of frosting. Heat the mixture, stirring until the sugar melts and cooks to a dark brown caramel. Pour onto a greased marble slab or baking sheet. When cold and crisp, pound the praline in a mortar and pestle or grind it in a rotary cheese grater and beat it into the frosting.

Raspberry
Framboise

1 cup butter cream frosting
½ cup puréed raspberries
1 ½ tablespoon kirsch

2.5 dl de crème au beurre
1.25 dl de purée de framboises
½-1 cuiller à soupe de kirsch

Purée fresh raspberries or thoroughly drained frozen raspberries
by working them through a sieve or puréeing them in a blender
and straining to remove seeds. Gradually beat the purée into butter
cream, allowing ½ cup purée to every cup of butter cream. Add
½-1 tablespoon kirsch to taste.

Strawberry
Fraise

1 cup butter cream frosting
½ cup puréed strawberries
1 ½ tablespoon kirsch

2.5 dl de crème au beurre
1.25 dl de purée de fraises
½-1 cuiller à soupe de kirsch

Purée fresh strawberries in a blender or work them through a sieve.
Gradually beat the purée into butter cream, allowing ½ cup purée to
every cup of butter cream, and add ½-1 tablespoon kirsch.

FLAVORINGS *for* BUTTER CREAM FROSTING *(continued)*
Parfums pour la Crème au Beurre *(suite)*

Vanilla
Vanille

1 cup butter cream frosting
1 teaspoon vanilla

> *2.5 dl de crème au beurre*
> *1 cuiller à café de vanille*

Into every cup of butter cream beat 1 teaspoon vanilla.

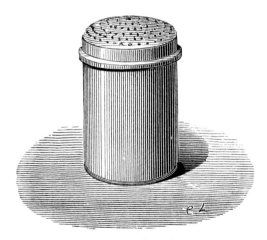

Sugar sifter. *Boîte a glacer.*

PASTRY CREAM
Crème Pâtissière

	1¼ CUPS PASTRY CREAM	1¾ CUPS PASTRY CREAM	2¼ CUPS PASTRY CREAM
egg yolks	3	5	6
sugar	4 T.	6 T.	8 T.
flour	2½ T.	4 T.	5 T.
milk	1 cup	1½ cups	2 cups
salt (optional)	pinch	pinch	pinch
vanilla bean (optional)	1	1	1

	3 DL DE CRÈME ENVIRON	*4.5 DL DE CRÈME ENVIRON*	*5.5 DL DE CRÈME ENVIRON*
jaunes d'oeufs	*3*	*5*	*6*
de sucre	*60 g*	*90 g*	*125 g*
de farine	*25 g*	*40 g*	*50 g*
de lait	*2.5 dl*	*4 dl*	*5 dl*
de sel (facultatif)	*pincée*	*pincée*	*pincée*
gousse de vanille (facultatif)	*1*	*1*	*1*

Beat the egg yolks with the sugar until thick and light. Stir in the flour and enough cold milk to make a smooth paste. Scald the remaining milk with the salt. If using a vanilla bean, add it to the hot milk, cover and leave to infuse 10-15 minutes. Remove the bean and wash it to use it again. Reheat the milk to boiling.

Whisk the boiling milk into the egg mixture, blend, return to the pan, and whisk over gentle heat until boiling. **NOTE:** Be sure the pastry cream is smooth before letting it boil. If lumps form as it thickens, take the pan from the heat and beat until smooth.

Cook the cream gently, whisking constantly, for 2 minutes or until the cream thins slightly showing the flour is completely cooked.

PASTRY CREAM *(continued)*
Crème Pâtissière (suite)

NOTE: Lightly cooked pastry cream tastes unpleasantly of flour. If the cream is too stiff, add a little milk. Take it from the heat, transfer the cream to a bowl and rub a piece of butter over the surface to prevent a skin from forming. Cover only after it has cooled.

Pastry cream can be stored, tightly covered, in the refrigerator for a day or two. Thick pastry cream can be frozen but if it is thin, it will separate.

Molded charlotte with Bavarian cream. *Charlotte russe.*

FLAVORINGS *for* PASTRY CREAM
Parfums de Crème Pâtissière

Chocolate
Chocolat

1 cup pastry cream
2-3 squares (2-3 oz.) semisweet chocolate

2.5 dl de crème pâtissière
60-90 g de chocolat à croquer

To every cup of pastry cream add 2-3 squares (2-3 oz) semisweet chocolate, chopped and melted over hot water.

Coffee
Café

1 cup pastry cream
2-3 teaspoons dry instant coffee
1 tablespoon hot water

2.5 dl de crème pâtissière
2-3 cuillers à café de café soluble dissout dans 1 cuiller à soupe
  d'eau chaude

To every cup of pastry cream add 2-3 teaspoons dry instant coffee dissolved in 1 tablespoon hot water.

Liqueur
Liqueur

1 cup pastry cream
1-2 tablespoons liqueur such as kirsch or Grand Marnier

2.5 dl de crème pâtissière
1-2 cuillers à soupe de liqueur tel que kirsch ou Grand Marnier

To every cup of pastry cream add 1-2 tablespoons liqueur such as kirsch or Grand Marnier.

CUSTARD SAUCE
Crème Anglaise

	1¼ CUPS SAUCE	2¼ CUPS SAUCE	3½ CUPS SAUCE
milk	1 cup	2 cups	3 cups
vanilla bean (optional)	1	1	1
egg yolks	3	6	9
sugar	2 T.	4 T.	6 T.

	3 DL DE CRÈME	5.5 DL DE CRÈME	8 DL DE CRÈME
de lait	2.5 dl	5 dl	7.5 dl
gousse de vanille (facultatif)	1	1	1
jaunes d'oeufs	3	6	9
de sucre	30 g	60 g	90 g

Some cooks like to make custard sauce in a double boiler to ensure it does not get too hot and curdle. It can be served hot or cold, flavored with vanilla, lemon or orange rind, or liqueur.

Bring the milk almost to a boil with the vanilla bean, if using, and leave in a warm place to infuse for 10-15 minutes. Remove the bean, wash it to use again, and reheat the milk to boiling. Beat the egg yolks with the sugar until thick and light. Whisk in half the hot milk and whisk the mixture back into the remaining milk. Heat gently, stirring constantly with a wooden spoon, until custard thickens slightly; if you draw a finger across the back of the spoon, it will leave a clear trail. **NOTE:** Do not overcook or boil or it will curdle.

Take the custard from the heat at once and strain it into a bowl. If serving cold, let cool completely, cover tightly and chill. The custard can be kept up to 2 days in the refrigerator.

FONDANT
Fondant

	1 CUP FONDANT	2 CUPS FONDANT
sugar	1 cup	2 cups
water	½ cup	1 cup
corn syrup or glucose, or pinch of cream of tartar dissolved in 1 T. water, or ½ teaspoon lemon juice or vinegar	1 T.	2 T.
flavoring	Few drops flavoring such as almond or mint extract or ½-1 teaspoon vanilla (optional)	

	2.5 DL DE FONDANT	5 DL DE FONDANT
de sucre	250 g	500 g
d'eau	1.25 dl	2.5 dl
de glucose, ou une pincée de crème de tartre dissoute dans 1 cuiller à café d'eau ou ½ cuiller à café de jus de citron ou de vinaigre	25 g	50 g
pour parfumer	Des gouttes d'extrait d'amandes ou de menthe ou ½-1 cuiller à café de vanille	

FONDANT *(continued)*
Fondant (suite)

In a heavy based pan, heat sugar and water until dissolved. Add corn syrup, glucose, dissolved cream of tartar, lemon juice, or vinegar. Bring to a boil and boil steadily without stirring to the soft ball stage (239°F/115°C on a sugar thermometer). If crystals form on sides of pan during boiling, wash down with a brush dipped in water. Take pan at once from heat, add flavoring, let the bubbles subside, and pour the mixture slowly, from a height, into a dampened tray. Sprinkle with a little water to prevent a crust from forming.

When cool, remove mixture with a sugar scraper to a cool marble slab. Pull the mixture together, using a sugar scraper or metal spatula and taking mixture from edge to center. Keep working fondant vigorously with a sugar scraper, turning and pulling to the center until it becomes white and creamy—it will do this suddenly and become too stiff to work. If fondant gets very hard and seems impossible to work, place an overturned bowl over it for a few minutes; the humidity will soften the fondant and it can be worked further.

Take a small piece of fondant at a time and work with the fingers until smooth. Pack into an airtight container and let stand at least 1 hour and preferably 2-3 days to mellow. Fondant can be kept in an airtight container for up to 1 year.

ROYAL ICING
Glaçage Royale

1½ cups confectioner's sugar
1 egg white
½ teaspoon vinegar or lemon juice

Makes about 1 cup icing.

200 g de sucre glace
1 blanc d'oeuf
½ cuiller à café de vinaigre ou de jus de citron

Rendement: 2.5 dl de glaçage environ.

Mix all of the ingredients together until well incorporated. Then with a wooden spoon, beat the mixture until fairly stiff peaks are formed. If not using immediately, cover with a damp cloth to prevent a crust from forming.

Crêpe pan. *Poêle à crêpes.*

GLACE ICING
Glaçage Simple

About 1½ cups confectioner's sugar
½ teaspoon vanilla,
   or 1 teaspoon instant coffee dissolved in 1 tablespoon warm water,
   or 1 square (1 oz) semisweet chocolate,
   or 2-3 tablespoons lemon or orange juice,
   or 1-2 tablespoons kirsch, rum or liqueur (for flavoring)
1-4 tablespoons of water
Edible food coloring (optional)

Makes about 1 cup icing.

Environ 200 g de sucre glace environ
½ cuiller à café de vanille,
   ou 1 cuiller à café de café soluble dissout
     dans 1 cuiller à soupe d'eau tiède,
   ou 30 g de chocolat à croquer,
   ou 2-3 cuillers à soupe de jus d'orange ou de citron,
   ou 1-2 cuillers à soupe de kirsch, de rhum ou de liqueur (pour
   parfumer)
1-4 cuillers à soupe d'eau
Colorant (facultatif)

Rendement: 2.5 dl de glaçage environ.

Sift confectioner's sugar into a bowl. If using chocolate, chop, melt
on a heatproof plate over a pan of hot water and cool. Add chocolate
or chosen flavoring to sugar with 1-2 tablespoons water. Mix to
a smooth, stiff paste. Set bowl in a pan of hot water and heat to
lukewarm; icing should be thick enough to coat the back of a spoon.
If too thick, add more water; if too thin, beat in more confectioner's
sugar. Add coloring if using—icing should be delicately, not brightly
colored. Use at once while warm.

SWISS MERINGUE
Meringue Suisse

4 egg whites
1¼ cups sugar
1 teaspoon vanilla (optional)

> *4 blancs d'oeufs*
> *240 g de sucre*
> *1 cuiller à café de vanille (facultatif)*
>
> *Rendement: 6 dl environ.*

Swiss meringue is used for meringue toppings, meringues Chantilly and sometimes for meringue cases such as vacherin. The recipe makes about 2½ cups meringue.

Stiffly whip the egg whites, if possible using a copper bowl. Add 4 teaspoons of the sugar and continue beating ½-1 minute until the egg whites are slightly glossy. Fold in the remaining sugar, adding a few tablespoons at a time. Fold in the vanilla with the last spoonful of sugar. **NOTE:** Do not overmix or the meringue will become liquid as the sugar dissolves.

Swiss meringue can be kept up to an hour in the refrigerator, covered with a damp cloth, but afterwards it will start to separate.

COOKED MERINGUE
Meringue Cuite

2⅓ cups confectioner's sugar
5 egg whites
1 teaspoon vanilla (optional)

> *300 g de sucre glace*
> *5 blancs d'oeufs*
> *1 cuiller à café de vanille (facultatif)*
>
> *Rendement: 6 dl environ.*

Cooked meringue is the driest and closest-textured of all meringues. It is baked to make petits fours, and it is used in frostings and fillings, when it is not cooked further. The recipe makes about 2½ cups meringue.

Sift the confectioner's sugar. Have ready a pan half full of simmering water. In a bowl, preferably of copper, beat the egg whites until frothy. Beat in the confectioner's sugar a tablespoon at a time, and then add the vanilla. Set the bowl over hot water and continue beating until the mixture forms a tall peak when the whisk is lifted. Take from heat and continue whisking until cool. An electric hand mixer can be used.

Cooked meringue can be kept covered in the refrigerator for up to a week.

ITALIAN MERINGUE
Meringue Italienne

1 cup sugar
½ cup water
4 egg whites
1 teaspoon vanilla (optional)

240 g de sucre
1.25 dl d'eau
4 blancs d'oeufs
1 cuiller à café de vanille (facultatif)

Rendement: 6 dl environ.

Italian meringue has a somewhat drier texture than Swiss meringue and holds up much longer. It is used in petits fours, as a frosting and is added to butter cream. The recipe makes about 2½ cups meringue.

Heat the sugar with the water over low heat until dissolved. Bring to a boil and boil without stirring until the syrup reaches the hard ball stage (248°F/120°C on a sugar thermometer). **NOTE:** While boiling, wash down any sugar crystals from the sides of the pan with a brush dipped in water. Meanwhile, stiffly whip the egg whites. Gradually pour in the hot sugar syrup, whisking constantly, and continue whisking until the meringue is cold—it will be stiff and glossy. Beat in the vanilla.

Italian meringue can be kept covered in the refrigerator up to a week.

CHAPTER 5

ICE CREAMS, SHERBETS, AND POACHED FRUIT

Les Glaces, Sorbets, et Fruits Pochés

French pastry chefs delight in the versatility of ice creams, sorbets, and molded bombes. Today's flavorings range far beyond familiar vanilla, coffee, chocolate and pistachio to include exotic fruit and spices. Sorbets are often based on purées of soft fresh fruit or fruit that has been poached in sugar syrup until tender. The term compote refers to poached fruit that is served in its cooking syrup, usually at room temperature. Cookies, a slice of cake, crème fraîche, yogurt, or ice cream are favorite accompaniments.

BASIC ICE CREAM
Recette de Base pour Glace

Chosen flavoring (see following pages)
2 cups milk
5 egg yolks
⅔ cup sugar
1 cup heavy cream, whipped until it holds a soft shape

Makes about 1 quart ice cream.

Parfum au choix (voir ci-dessous)
5 dl de lait
5 jaunes d'oeufs
125 g de sucre
2.5 dl de crème fraîche, légèrement fouettée

Rendement: 1 litre environ de glace.

Prepare the chosen flavoring as described below.

Bring the milk almost to a boil. Beat the egg yolks with the sugar until thick and light. Whisk in half the hot milk and whisk the mixture back into the remaining milk. Heat gently, stirring constantly with a wooden spoon, until the custard thickens slightly; if you draw your finger across the back of the spoon, it will leave a clear trail.
NOTE: Do not overcook or boil the custard or it will curdle.

Take the custard at once from the heat and strain it into a bowl. Let cool and pour into a churn freezer. When the ice cream is partly set, add the whipped cream to the mixture and continue freezing in the churn freezer until set.

FLAVORINGS *for* ICE CREAM
Parfums pour les Glaces

Chocolate
Chocolat

7 squares (7 oz) semisweet chocolate

200 g de chocolat à croquer

Melt 7 squares (7 oz) semisweet chocolate, chopped, over hot water and add to the custard before straining.

Coffee I
Café I

¼ cup medium ground coffee

25 g de café moyennement moulu

Heat the milk with ¼ cup medium-ground coffee, cover, and infuse 10-15 minutes. Strain the milk and bring back to a boil before adding it to the egg yolk mixture.

Coffee II
Café II

1-1 ½ tablespoons dry instant coffee

1-1½ cuillers à soupe de café soluble

Scald the milk and add 1-1½ tablespoons dry instant coffee. Whisk the hot milk into the egg yolk mixture.

FLAVORINGS *for* ICE CREAM *(continued)*
Parfums pour les Glaces (suite)

Praline
Praliné

¼ cup sugar
⅓ cup whole almonds
1 vanilla bean

60 g de sucre
60 g d'amandes
1 gousse de vanille

To make praline: In a heavy based pan, heat ¼ cup sugar and ⅓ cup whole blanched or unblanched almonds, stirring occasionally, until the sugar melts and starts to caramelize. Continue cooking over low heat, stirring, until the mixture is deep brown and the almonds pop, showing they are toasted. **NOTE:** Do not allow the caramel to burn. Immediately pour the mixture onto an oiled baking sheet and let it cool and harden. When crisp, work it to a powder a little at a time in a blender or rotary cheese grater. Heat the milk with a vanilla bean, cover and infuse 10-15 minutes. Strain the milk and bring back to a boil before adding to the egg yolk mixture. After straining the custard, stir in the powdered praline.

Pistachio
Pistache

1 cup shelled pistachios
2-3 tablespoons heavy cream

150 g de pistaches
2-3 cuillers à soupe de crème fraîche

Blanch 1 cup shelled pistachios in boiling water, drain, and peel them.
Pound them in a mortar and pestle or work them in a blender with
2-3 tablespoons heavy cream to make a smooth paste. Heat the milk
with the pistachio paste, cover, and leave to infuse 10-15 minutes.
Strain the milk and bring back to a boil before adding it to the egg
yolk mixture; lightly color it with a few drops green food coloring.

Vanilla
Vanille

Replace sugar with vanilla sugar
1 vanilla bean (or 1 ½ teaspoons essence)

Remplacer le sucre par du sucre vanille
1 gousse de vanille (ou 1½ cuillers à café extrait de vanille)

If possible, beat the egg yolks with vanilla sugar (made by leaving a
vanilla bean in the sugar in an airtight container) instead of regular
sugar. Heat the milk with a vanilla bean, cover, and leave to infuse
10-15 minutes. Strain the milk and bring back to a boil before adding
it to the egg yolk mixture. (If vanilla essence is used instead of a
vanilla bean, add 1½ teaspoons essence after the custard is cool.)

Sherbet
Sorbet

Sherbets are made with fruit juice or purée, sweet or sparkling wine, and are sweetened with sugar syrup. Sherbets must always be sweetened to taste as the amount of sugar needed varies enormously with the acidity of the fruit or wine. A small quantity of lightly beaten egg white can be added to sherbet halfway through freezing to lighten the mixture.

Sugar Syrup for Sherbet
Sirop pour les Sorbets

1¾ cups sugar
1 cup water
Juice of ½ lemon

Makes about 1¼ cups syrup.

> *350 g de sucre*
> *2.5 dl d'eau*
> *Le jus d'un ½ citron*
>
> *Rendement: 3 dl de sirop environ.*

Heat the sugar with the water and lemon juice over low heat until dissolved, then boil just until the syrup is clear, or about 2-3 minutes.

CHAMPAGNE SHERBET
Sorbet au Champagne

½ cup cool sugar syrup
1 bottle (about 3 cups) Champagne
2⅓ cups water
½ egg white, beaten until frothy (optional)

1.5 dl de sirop
1 bouteille (7.2 dl) de Champagne
6 dl d'eau
½ blanc d'oeuf (facultatif)

Rendement: 1.5 litres de sorbet.

Any other sparkling wine such as Asti Spumante or Vouvray can be used in this recipe.

To ½ cup cool sugar syrup add 1 bottle (about 3 cups) of Champagne and 2⅓ cups water. Taste the mixture, adding more syrup if needed. Freeze in a churn freezer until slushy and, if you like, add ½ egg white, beaten until frothy. Continue freezing until firm. Serve in chilled sherbet glasses.

Makes about 1½ quarts sherbet.

LEMON SHERBET
Sorbet au Citron

1¼ cups sugar syrup
Zest of 4 lemons
1 cup fresh lemon juice (from about 5-6 lemons)
3 cups water
½ egg white, beaten until frothy (optional)

5 dl de sirop
Le zeste râpé de 4 citrons
2.5 dl de jus de citron (environ 5-6 citrons)
7.5 dl d'eau, ½ blanc d'oeuf (facultatif)

Rendement: 1.25 litres de sorbet.

To 1¼ cups sugar syrup add the grated rind of 4 lemons, 1 cup fresh lemon juice (from about 5-6 lemons), and 3 cups water. Taste and add more syrup or lemon juice if necessary. Freeze in a churn freezer until slushy and, if you like, add ½ egg white, beaten until frothy. Continue freezing until firm. Serve in chilled sherbet glasses. Alternatively, pack the sherbet into hollowed lemon shells and cover with the lid to make citrons givrées. Top each lemon with a lemon or bay leaf just before serving.

Makes about 1¼ quarts sherbet or 5-6 filled lemons.

MINT SHERBET
Sorbet à la Menthe

1 cup crushed mint leaves

50 g de feuilles de menthe écrasées, infusées dans le sirop

Suivez la recette du sorbet au citron

In the recipe for lemon sherbet, add 1 cup crushed mint leaves to the hot sugar syrup and infuse, covered, over low heat for 10-15 minutes. Cool, strain, and continue as for lemon sherbet. Mint sherbet can be served as a light appetizer for summer, particularly when made less sweet.

Copper bowl for whisking egg whites. *Bassine à blanc d'oeuf en cuivre avec fouet.*

ORANGE SHERBET
Sorbet à l'Orange

⅔ cup sugar syrup
Zest of 6 oranges
3 cups fresh orange juice (from about 10-12 oranges)
Juice of ½ lemon
⅓ cup water
½ egg white, beaten until frothy (optional)

> *2 dl de sirop*
> *Le zeste râpé de 6 oranges*
> *7.5 dl de jus d'orange (environ 10-12 oranges)*
> *Le jus d'un ½ citron*
> *1 dl d'eau*
> *½ blanc d'oeuf (facultatif)*
>
> *Rendement: 1 litre de sorbet.*

To ⅔ cup sugar syrup add the grated rind of 6 oranges, 3 cups fresh orange juice (from about 10-12 oranges), the juice of ½ lemon, and ⅓ cup water. Taste and add more syrup or lemon juice if necessary. Freeze in a churn freezer until slushy and, if you like, add ½ egg white, beaten until frothy. Continue freezing until firm. Serve in chilled sherbet glasses. Makes about 1 quart sherbet.

PINEAPPLE SHERBET
Sorbet à l'Ananas

Flesh of a large pineapple
1 cup sugar syrup
1 cup water
Juice of 1 lemon
2-3 tablespoons kirsch
½ egg white, beaten until frothy (optional)

La pulpe d'un gros ananas
2.5 dl de sirop, 2.5 dl d'eau
Le jus d'un citron
2 cuillers à soupe de kirsch
½ blanc d'oeuf (facultatif)

Rendement: 1 litre de sorbet.

Cut the plume and base from a large pineapple and slice the flesh, discarding the core. Pull the flesh into shreds with 2 forks or purée it in a blender. Add 1 cup sugar syrup, 1 cup water, the juice of 1 lemon, and 2 tablespoons kirsch and taste, adding more syrup if necessary. Freeze in a churn freezer until slushy and, if you like, add ½ egg white, beaten until frothy. Continue freezing until firm. Serve in sherbet glasses and, if you like, spoon over 1 tablespoon kirsch just before serving. Alternatively, the pineapple can be prepared by halving the fruit lengthwise, including the plume, and scooping out the flesh to make sherbet, reserving the shells for serving. Just before serving, scoop the sherbet into balls with an ice cream scoop and pile the balls in the chilled shells. If desired, the sherbet can be piled on a layer of strawberries, halved, and macerated in kirsch and sugar. Makes about 1 quart sherbet.

RASPBERRY SHERBET
Sorbet à la Framboise

1 quart raspberries
⅔ cup sugar syrup
1 cup water
1 tablespoon kirsch or the juice of ½ lemon
½ egg white, beaten until frothy (optional)

> *500 g de framboises*
> *2 dl de sirop*
> *2.5 dl d'eau*
> *1 cuiller à soupe de kirsch ou le jus d'un ½ citron*
> *½ blanc d'oeuf (facultatif)*
>
> *Rendement: 1 litre de sorbet.*

Purée 1 quart raspberries in a blender and strain to remove the seeds. Add ⅔ cup sugar syrup, 1 cup water, and 1 tablespoon kirsch or the juice of ½ lemon and taste the mixture, adding more syrup if necessary. Freeze in a churn freezer until slushy and, if you like, add ½ egg white, beaten until frothy. Continue freezing until firm. Serve in sherbet glasses. Makes about 1 quart sherbet.

Eggs in a basket. *Oeufs dans un calbanon.*

SECRETS *from the* LA VARENNE KITCHEN

STRAWBERRY SHERBET
Sorbet à la Fraise

1 quart hulled strawberries
⅔ cup sugar syrup
1 cup water
Juice of 1 lemon
1 tablespoon kirsch (optional)
½ egg white, beaten until frothy (optional)

> *500 g de fraises*
> *2 dl de sirop*
> *2.5 dl d'eau*
> *Le jus d'un citron*
> *1 cuiller à soupe de kirsch (facultatif)*
> *½ blanc d'oeuf (facultatif)*
>
> *Rendement: 1 litre de sorbet.*

Purée 1 quart hulled strawberries in a blender or work them through a food mill. Add ⅔ cup sugar syrup, 1 cup water, the juice of 1 lemon, and 1 tablespoon kirsch (optional). Taste the mixture, adding more syrup if necessary. Freeze in a churn freezer until slushy and, if you like, add ½ egg white, beaten until frothy. Continue freezing until firm. Serve alone in sherbet glasses or set a ball of sherbet on a slice of fresh pineapple. Makes about 1 quart sherbet.

SAUTERNES SHERBET
Sorbet au Sauternes

⅔ cup sugar syrup
⅔ cup sweet white wine
2¾ cups water
½ egg white, beaten until frothy (optional)

> *2 dl de sirop*
> *2 dl de Sauternes*
> *7 dl d'eau*
> *½ blanc d'oeuf (facultatif)*
>
> *Rendement: 1 litre de sorbet.*

Any sweet white wine, such as Tokay or Muscat, can be used in
this recipe.

To ⅔ cup sugar syrup add ⅔ cup sweet white wine and 2¾ cups
water. Taste the mixture adding more syrup or lemon juice to taste.
Freeze in a churn freezer until slushy and, if you like, add ½ egg white,
beaten until frothy. Continue freezing until firm. Serve in sherbet
glasses. Makes 1 quart sherbet.

TANGERINE SHERBET
Sorbet à la Mandarine

Follow basic recipe for orange sherbet
Grated rind of 10 tangerines
3 cups of juice (you'll need 18-20 tangerines)

> *suivez la recette du sorbet à l'orange*
> *le zeste râpé de 10 mandarines*
> *7.5 dl de jus de mandarine (environ 18-20 mandarines)*
>
> *Rendement: 1 litre de sorbet.*

Follow the recipe for orange sherbet, using the grated rind of 10 tangerines. You'll need about 18-20 tangerines to obtain 3 cups of juice. For filled tangerines or mandarines givrées, scoop out the flesh of the tangerines and reserve the shells. Pack the sherbet into the reserved shells, filling them well, and cover with the lids. Makes about 1 quart sherbet or 8-10 filled tangerines.

Unmolding Bavarian cream. *Démoulage de bavarois.*

POACHED FRUIT
Fruits Pochés

1 pound fruit (see below)
½ cup sugar or to taste
2 cups water
1 vanilla bean
Pared rind and juice of 1 lemon

> *500 g de fruits (voir ci-dessous)*
> *100 g de sucre ou selon goût*
> *5 dl d'eau*
> *1 gousse de vanille*
> *Le zeste pelé et le jus d'un citron*

Any of the fruits below, or a mixture of them, are suitable for poaching. They should be juicy, but firm and not too ripe.

Prepare the fruit (see below). In a saucepan, heat the sugar with the water, vanilla bean, lemon rind, and juice until the sugar is dissolved. Bring to a boil and add the prepared fruit. **NOTE:** The fruit should be completely covered by syrup and large halves or whole fruits, such as pears or peaches, may need cooking in 2 batches or in a double quantity of syrup. Place halved fruits cut side up in syrup so the rounded side is completely immersed. Bring the fruit almost back to a boil and poach gently until it is semi-transparent and just tender when pierced with the point of a small knife. Cooking time depends on the ripeness and variety of the fruit.

Let the fruit cool to tepid in the syrup, then transfer it to a glass serving bowl. Boil the syrup until fairly thick and reduced to 1-1½ cups. Let cool slightly, taste, add more sugar if needed and strain over the fruit. Serve cool or chilled.

FRUITS FOR POACHING
Fruits à Pocher

Apples

Dessert apples such as Golden Delicious are excellent for poaching, or tart cooking apples may be used. **NOTE:** Peel apples only just before cooking them and rub them immediately with a cut lemon, as they quickly discolor. Scoop out the stalk and flower end.

If serving whole: Core the apples and poach them, a few at a time, for 15-20 minutes, making sure that they are immersed in the syrup. For cut up apples: Halve them, scoop out the core and cut in quarters, if you like. Poach them a few at a time, for 8-12 minutes.

Pommes: entières, 15-20 minutes; moitiés ou quartiers, 8-12 minutes

Apricots

Cut around the apricots through the indentation, twist them in half, and discard the pits. Poach 5-8 minutes.

Abricots: 5-8 minutes

Cherries

Either sweet dark bing cherries or tart red cherries can be used. Poached tart cherries are often served with meat, poultry, or game, but they need more sugar if they are to be served as dessert. Wash the cherries, discard the stems and, if you like, remove the pits with a pitter or the point of a vegetable peeler. Poach the cherries 8-12 minutes.

Cerises: 8-12 minutes

FRUITS FOR POACHING (continued)
Fruits à Pocher (suite)

Cranberries

Pick over the cranberries and wash thoroughly. Make the sugar syrup with 1½ cups sugar. Add the berries and poach 4-5 minutes. They overcook easily. If serving for dessert, they tend to be sour and may need more sugar.

Airelles: sirop—300 g de sucre, 5 dl d'eau; 4-5 minutes

Pears

Firm pears such as Anjou or Bosc should be used for poaching.
NOTE: Pears discolor very rapidly and must be rubbed with a cut lemon and immersed in syrup as soon as they are peeled. If serving whole: Scoop out the flower end with the point of a knife and, if you like, insert a small sharp coffee spoon or the tip of a vegetable peeler into the pear to scoop out the core; peel the pear, leaving the stalk. Poach the pears, a few at a time, for 20-25 minutes, making sure that they are immersed in syrup. For cut up pears: Peel them, discarding the flower end, halve them, cut out the core and stem, and quarter or slice them. Poach 5-10 minutes.

Poires: entières 20-25 minutes; quartiers ou tranches 5-10 minutes

Plums

Make the sugar syrup with 1½ cups water. Cut around the plums through the indentation and twist them in half, discarding the pits, or leave them whole. Poach 8-12 minutes. Poached plums are particularly good served with a sprinkling of cinnamon.

Prunes: sirop—100 g de sucre, 3.75 dl d'eau; 8-12 minutes,
cannelle (facultatif)

Peaches

Cut around the peaches through the indentation, twist them in half and discard the pits. If desired, crack a few of the pits and use the kernels to give an almond flavor to the syrup. Poach the peaches, a few at a time, for 7-10 minutes. Let them cool to tepid, then peel them. Small peaches can also be poached whole: Poach them 15-20 minutes, let cool to tepid, and peel them. Poached white peaches are particularly good with brandy added.

Pêches: moitiés, 7-10 minutes; entières, 15-20 minutes, Cognac (facultatif)

Rhubarb

Make the sugar syrup with 1 cup water. Wash the rhubarb and cut in 2-inch lengths. Poach it 5-10 minutes; it overcooks very easily.

Rhubarbe: sirop—100 g de sucre, 2.5 dl d'eau; 5-10 minutes

Fruit. *Fruit.*

CHAPTER 6

COOKING with SUGAR

La Cuisson du Sucre

Cooking with sugar is a precise process
and starts with sugar syrup. The technical
description of each of the half-dozen stages
is summed up in their names: "soft ball,"
"hard crack," and so on. A sugar thermometer
is very helpful in identifying correct
temperatures, though with practice the
stages of boiling sugar can be spotted by eye
and with a hand test in a bowl of cold water.

COOKING SUGAR

The main differences between syrups and cooked sugars are in temperature and method of measurement.

While a syrup is brought only to a boil (214°F or 101°C), and cooked just long enough to completely dissolve the sugar in the water, a cooked sugar is cooked until it reaches higher temperatures. A hydrometer is used for syrups, while a candy or sugar thermometer is used for cooked sugar.

Syrups are often described by their density (degrees on the Baumé scale). A degree of density (specific gravity) measures the concentration, not the temperature, of the sugar solution. These degrees correspond to the given number on a hydrometer as shown in the table.

Dessert. *Dessert.*

A cooked sugar's structure differs according to the temperature to which it is cooked. The original proportions of water and sugar are not important because the water evaporates during the cooking process. To save time, it's best to start with just enough water to cover the sugar (about ⅓ the weight of the sugar in water). The stages of cooking sugar take their names from the hand tests used to determine whether the sugar is at the proper temperature for a specific purpose. **CAUTION:** Always dip your fingers in cold water before and immediately after putting them in the hot syrup. Never put your fingers in caramel. Alternatively, a sugar temperature thermometer can be used.

A chart of sugar syrup temperatures is on the next page.

Nougat. *Nougat.*

SUGAR COOKING CHART
Cuisson du Sucre

| NAME | PROPORTION SUGAR AND WATER | DEGREES | | TEMPERATURE |
| | | DENSITY | | |
		BAUME	HYDROMETER NUMBER	°C
	5¼ cups (1 kg) sugar 2 quarts (2 l) water	18°	1.1425	101°
Syrup *Sirop*	5¼ cups (1 kg) sugar 1 quart (1 l) water	25°	1.2095	101°
	5¼ cups (1 kg) sugar 3 cups (7.5 dl) water	30°	1.2624	101°
Soft Ball *Petit Boulé*	5¼ cups (1 kg) sugar 1¼ cups (3 dl) water			115°
Hard Ball *Gros Boulé*	5¼ cups (1 kg) sugar 1¼ cups (3 dl) water			120°
Light Crack *Petit Cassé*	5¼ cups (1 kg) sugar 1¼ cups (3 dl) water			125°
Hard Crack *Grand Cassé*	5¼ cups (1 kg) sugar 1¼ cups (3 dl) water			145°-146°
Caramel	5¼ cups (1 kg) sugar 1¼ cups (3 dl) water			165°-170°
Dark Caramel *Caramel Foncé*	5¼ cups (1 kg) sugar 1¼ cups (3 dl) water			190°

(vertical label: COOKED SUGAR / SUCRE CUIT)

TEMPERATURE °F	TESTING BY HAND	USE
214°		Soaking babas
214°		Moistening génoise, making candied fruits *(Fruits confits)*
214°		Making sherbet *(Sirop à sorbet)*
239°	Forms soft ball in cold water	Fondant, butter cream
248°	Forms firm ball Pliable in cold water	Italian meringue
257°	Brittle but sticks to teeth	Hard caramels *(Caramels durs)*
293°-295°	Very brittle Doesn't stick to teeth	Glazed fruits *(Fruits glacés)*, Glazing choux puffs *(Choux glacés)*, Angel's hair *(Cheveux d'ange)*, Pulled sgar *(Sucre tiré)*
329°-338°	Light to golden brown	Sauces, crème caramel, pralines
374°	Dark and smokes	Coloring

INDEX

INDEX *(continued)*